FOR ORGANS, PIANOS & ELECTRONIC KEYBOARD

ANDREW LLOYD WEBBER™ FAVORITES

ISBN 978-1-4234-8204-8

7777 W. Bluemound Rd. P.O. Box 13819 Milwaukee, WI 53213

Visit Hal Leonard Online at
www.halleonard.com

Another Suitcase in Another Hall

from EVITA

Registration 8
Rhythm: 4/4 Ballad or 8-Beat

Words by Tim Rice
Music by Andrew Lloyd Webber

N.C.
C F G C
I don't ex - pect my love af - fairs to last for long, nev - er
Time and time a - gain I've said that I don't care, that I'm im -
Call in three months' time and I'll be fine, I know. Well, may - be
F G7 G C G
fool my - self that my dreams will come true.
mune to gloom, that I'm hard through and through. But
not that fine, but I'll sur - vive an - y - how. I
C F G Am
Be - ing used to trou - ble I an - ti - ci - pate it, but
ev - 'ry time it mat - ters all my words de - sert me, so
won't re - call the names and plac - es of each sad oc - ca - sion, but
G F C
all the same I hate it, would - n't you?
an - y - one can hurt me and they do.
that's no con - so - la - tion here and now.
So what hap - pens

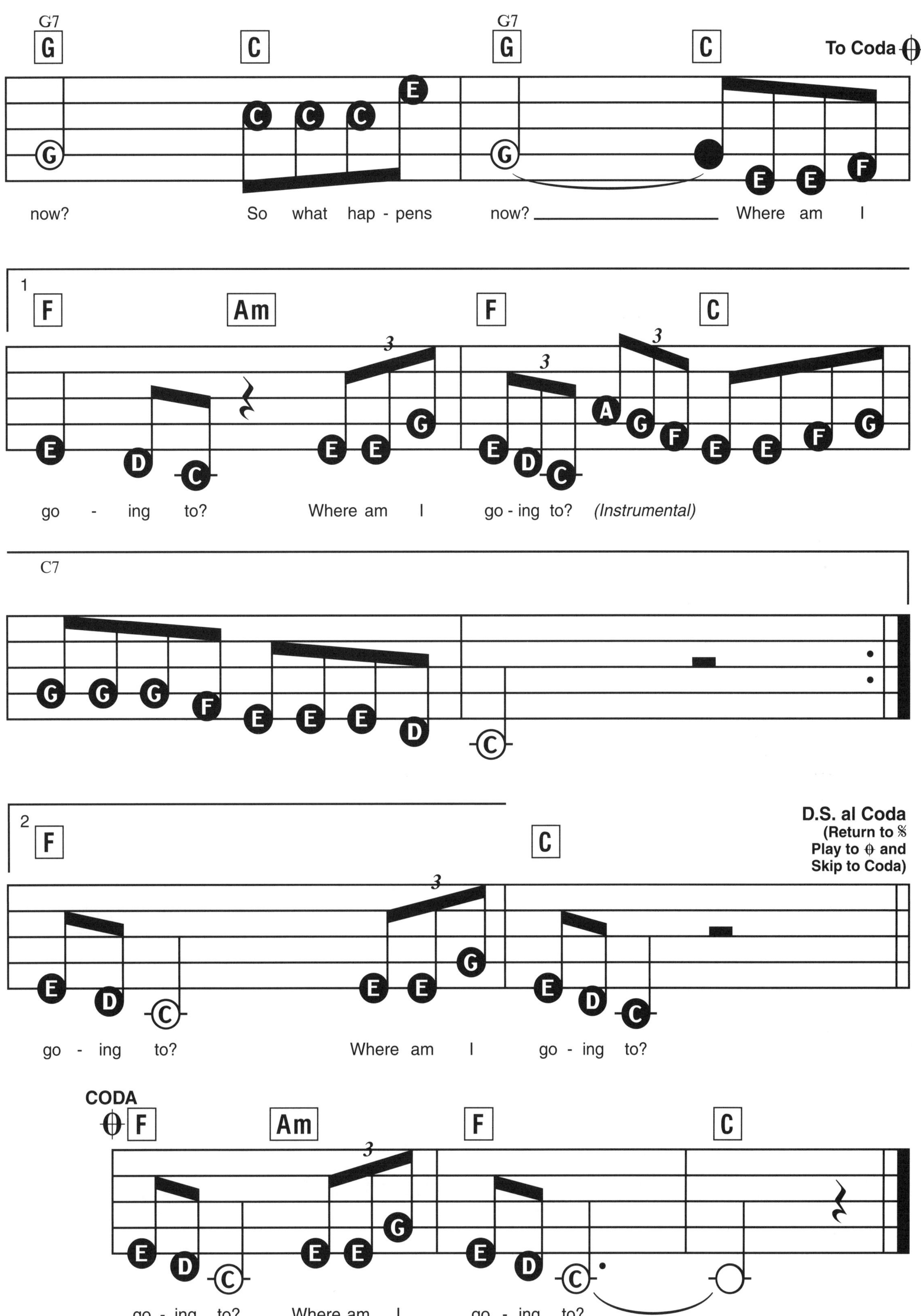
G7
G
C
G7
G
C
To Coda
now?
So what hap - pens
now?
Where am I
1
F
Am
F
C
go - ing to?
Where am I
go - ing to?
(Instrumental)
C7
2
F
C
D.S. al Coda
(Return to 𝄋
Play to 𝄌 and
Skip to Coda)
go - ing to?
Where am I
go - ing to?
CODA
F
Am
F
C
go - ing to?
Where am I
go - ing to?

Anything But Lonely

from ASPECTS OF LOVE

Registration 2
Rhythm: 4/4 Ballad

Music by Andrew Lloyd Webber
Lyrics by Don Black and Charles Hart

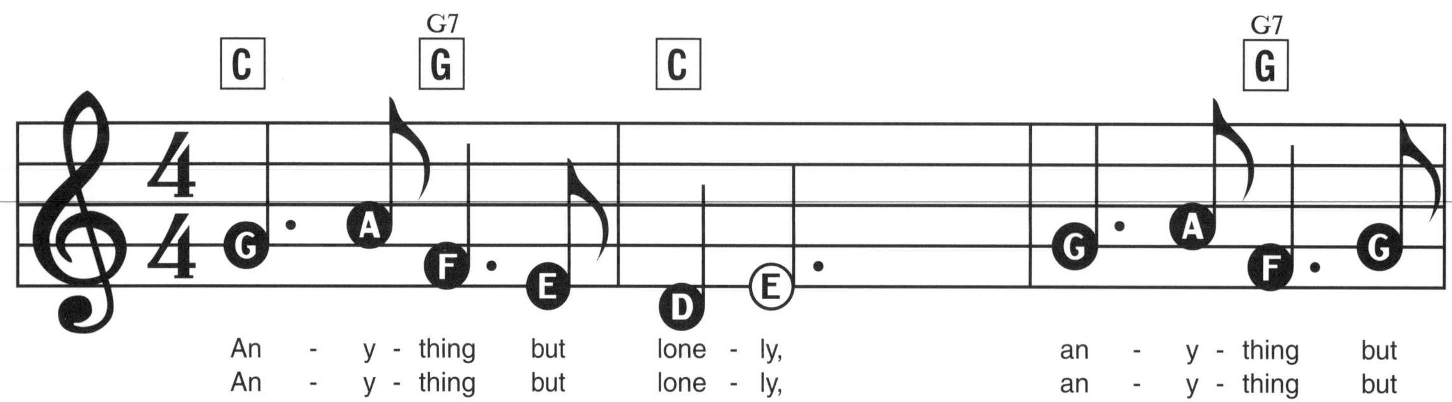

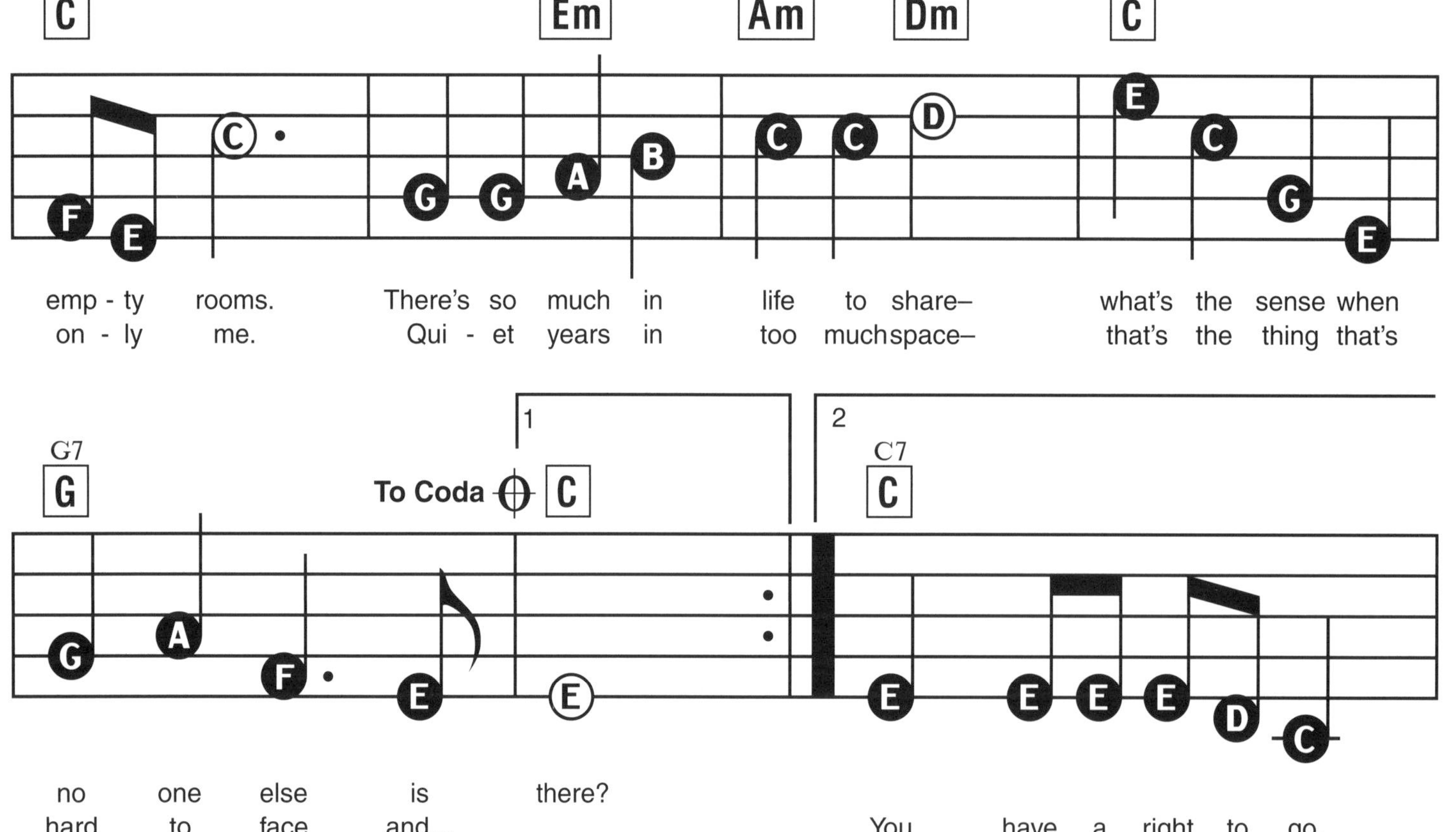

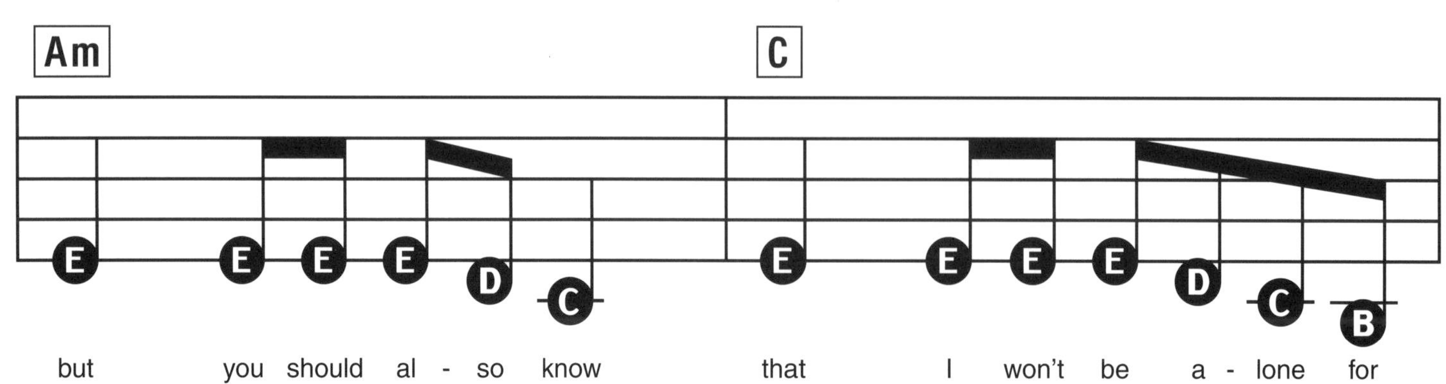

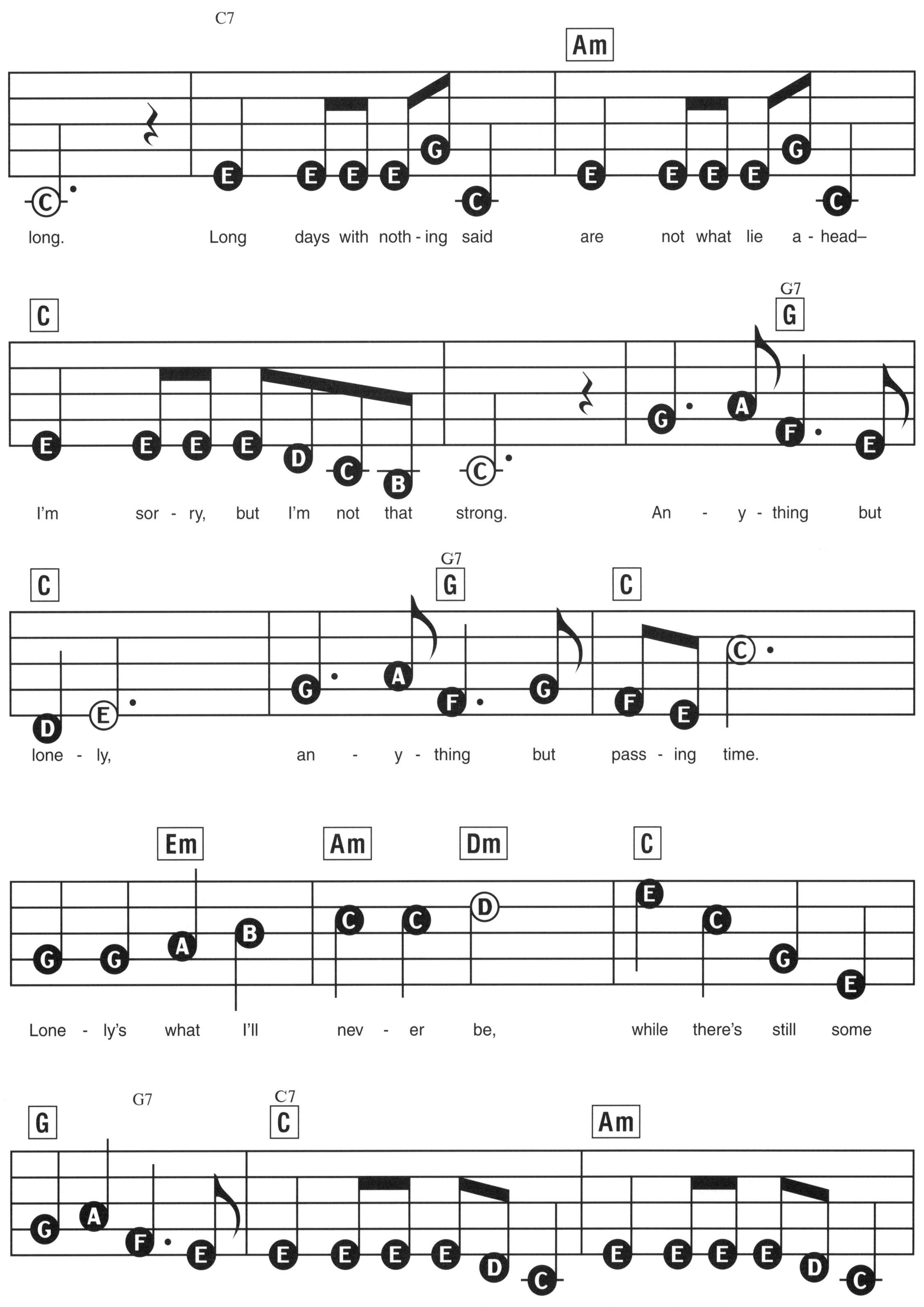

C7
Am
long. Long days with noth - ing said are not what lie a - head–
C
G7
G
I'm sor - ry, but I'm not that strong. An - y - thing but
C
G7
G
C
lone - ly, an - y - thing but pass - ing time.
Em
Am
Dm
C
Lone - ly's what I'll nev - er be, while there's still some
G
G7
C7
C
Am
life in me, and… I'm still young, don't for - get, it is - n't o - ver yet–

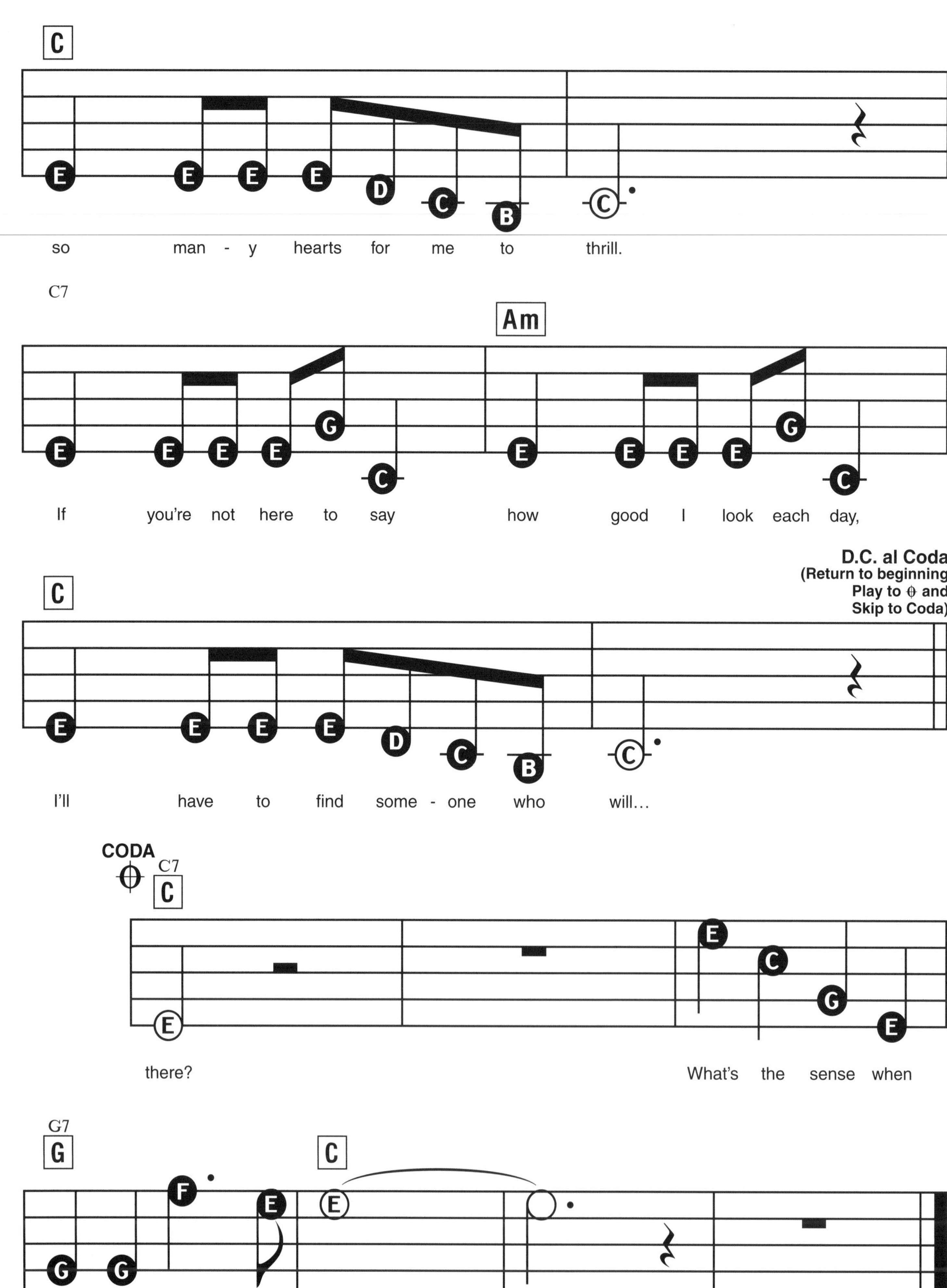
C
E E E E D C B C
so man - y hearts for me to thrill.
C7
Am
E E E E G C E E E E G C
If you're not here to say how good I look each day,
C
D.C. al Coda
(Return to beginning
Play to ⊕ and
Skip to Coda)
E E E E D C B C
I'll have to find some - one who will...
CODA
C7
C
E E C G E
there? What's the sense when
G7
G
C
G G F E E
no one else is there?

Close Every Door

from JOSEPH AND THE AMAZING TECHNICOLOR® DREAMCOAT

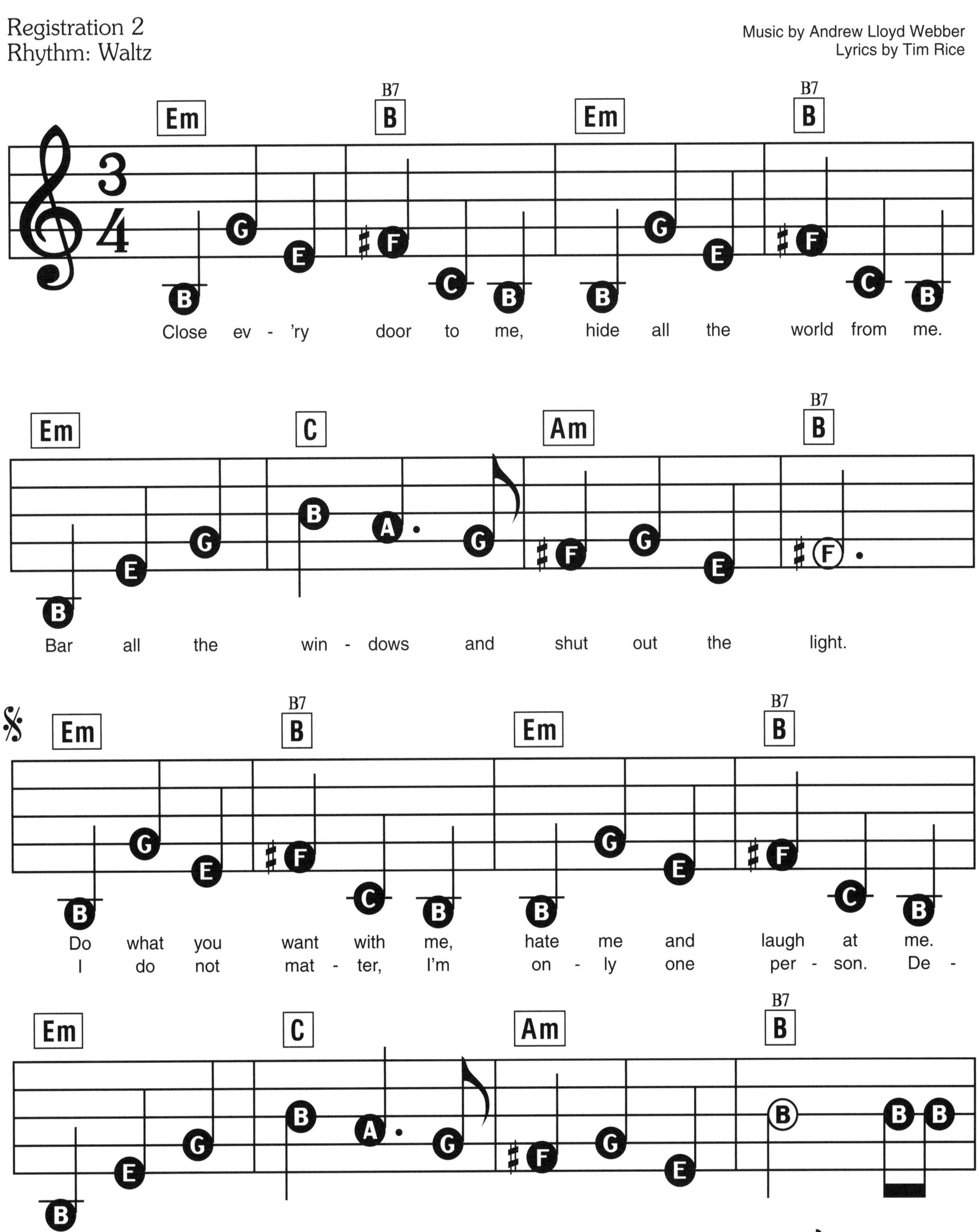
Registration 2
Rhythm: Waltz
Music by Andrew Lloyd Webber
Lyrics by Tim Rice
Em B7 B Em B7 B
Close ev - 'ry door to me, hide all the world from me.
Em C Am B7 B
Bar all the win - dows and shut out the light.
Em B7 B Em B7 B
Do what you want with me, hate me and laugh at me.
I do not mat - ter, I'm on - ly one per - son. De -
Em C Am B7 B
Dark - en my day - time and tor - ture my night.
stroy me com - plete - ly and throw me a - way.
If my

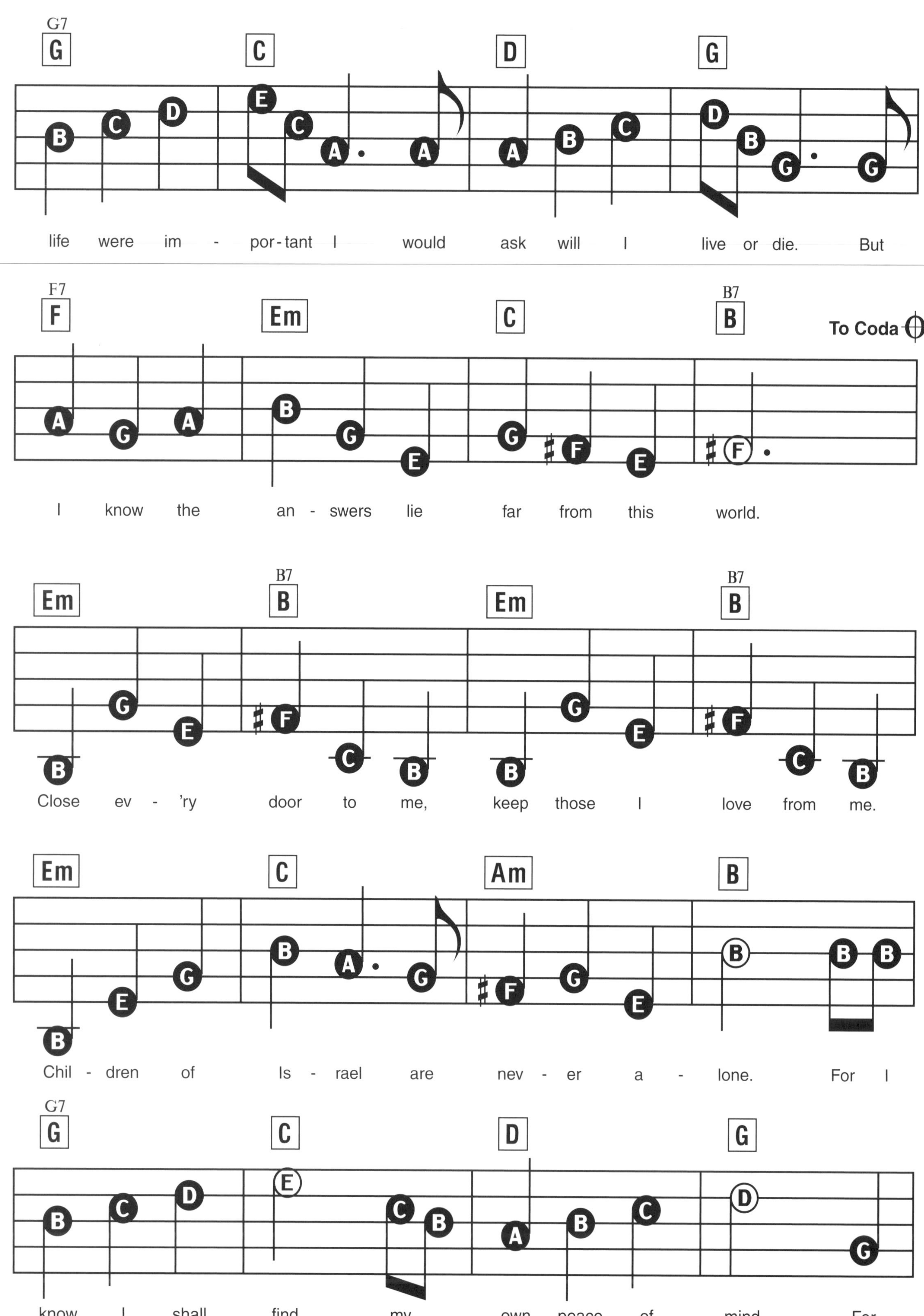
G7
G
C
D
G
B C D E C A A A B C D B G G
life were im - por-tant I would ask will I live or die. But
F7
F
Em
C
B7
B
To Coda
A G A B G E G F E F
I know the an - swers lie far from this world.
Em
B7
B
Em
B7
B
B G E F C B B G E F C B
Close ev - 'ry door to me, keep those I love from me.
Em
C
Am
B
B E G B A G F G E B B B
Chil - dren of Is - rael are nev - er a - lone. For I
G7
G
C
D
G
B C D E C B A B C D G
know I shall find, my own peace of mind. For

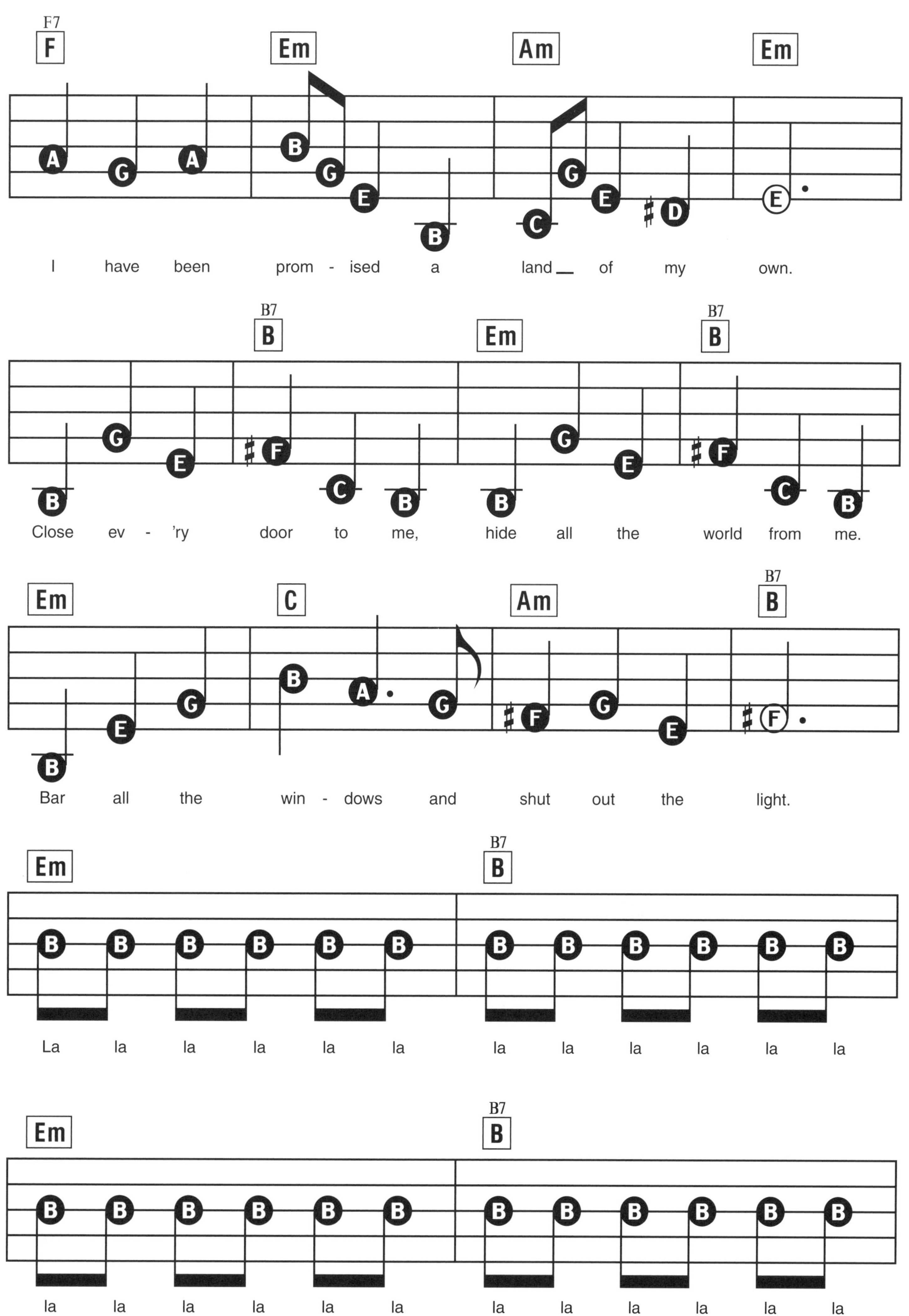
F7
F
Em
Am
Em
A G A B G E B C G E ♯D E
I have been prom - ised a land of my own.
B7
B
Em
B7
B
B G E ♯F C B B G E ♯F C B
Close ev - 'ry door to me, hide all the world from me.
Em
C
Am
B7
B
B E G B A G ♯F G E ♯F
Bar all the win - dows and shut out the light.
Em
B7
B
B B B B B B B B B B B B
La la la la la la la la la la la la
Em
B7
B
B B B B B B B B B B B B
la la la la la la la la la la la la

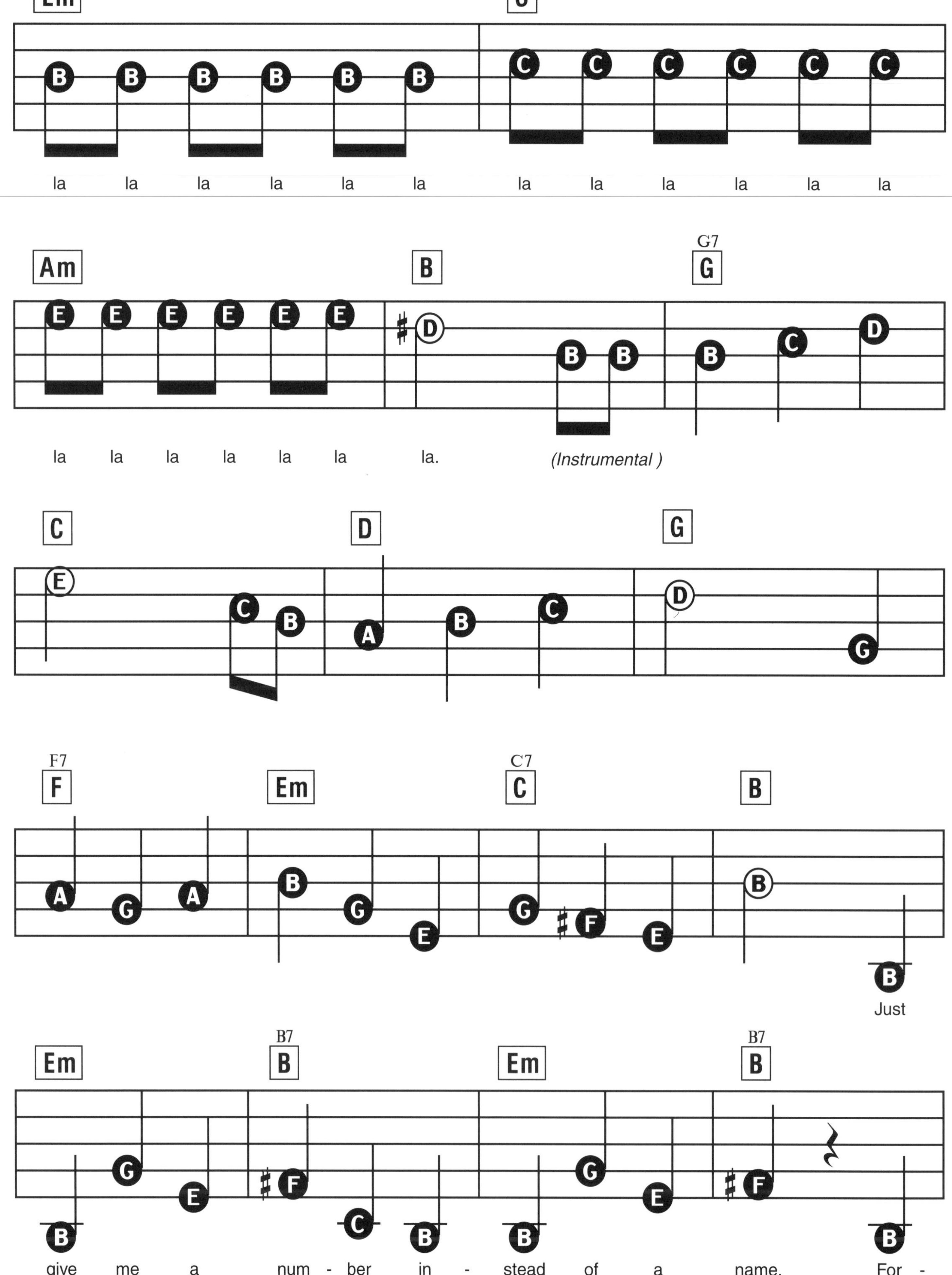
Em
B B B B B B
la la la la la la
C
C C C C C C
la la la la la la
Am
E E E E E E
la la la la la la
B
D B B
la.
(Instrumental)
G7
G
B C D
C
E C B
D
A B C
G
D G
F7
F
A G A
Em
B G E
C7
C
G F E
B
B B
Just
Em
B G E
give me a
B7
B
F C B
num - ber in -
Em
B G E
stead of a
B7
B
F B
name. For -

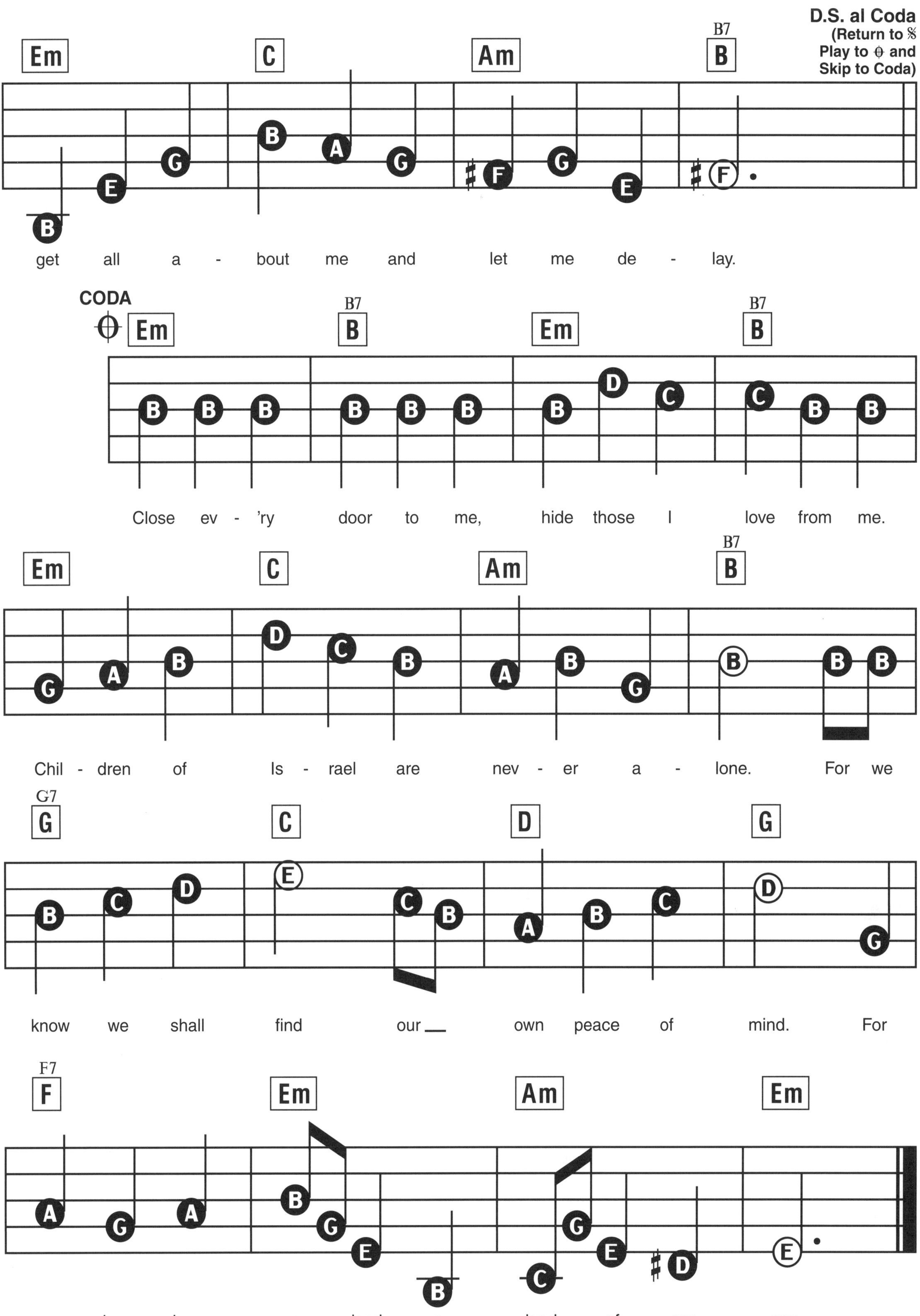
D.S. al Coda
(Return to 𝄋
Play to ⊕ and
Skip to Coda)
Em
C
Am
B7
B
get all a - bout me and let me de - lay.
CODA
Em
B7
B
Em
B7
B
Close ev - 'ry door to me, hide those I love from me.
Em
C
Am
B7
B
Chil - dren of Is - rael are nev - er a - lone. For we
G7
G
C
D
G
know we shall find our own peace of mind. For
F7
F
Em
Am
Em
we have been prom - ised a land of our own.

Crazy

from STARLIGHT EXPRESS

Registration 8
Rhythm: 8-Beat or Rock

Music by Andrew Lloyd Webber
Lyrics by Richard Stilgoe

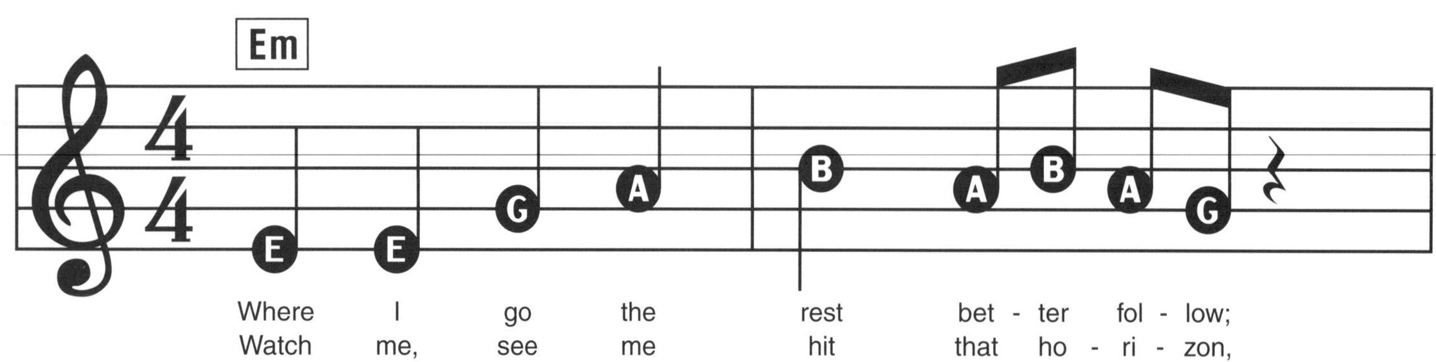
Em
E E G A B A B A G
Where I go the rest bet - ter fol - low;
Watch me, see me hit that ho - ri - zon,

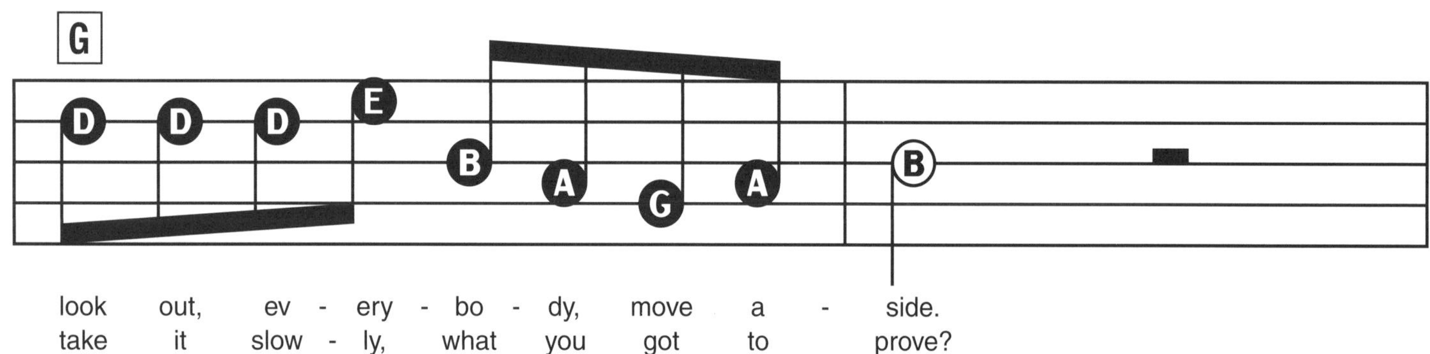
G
D D D E B A G A B
look out, ev - ery - bo - dy, move a - side.
take it slow - ly, what you got to prove?

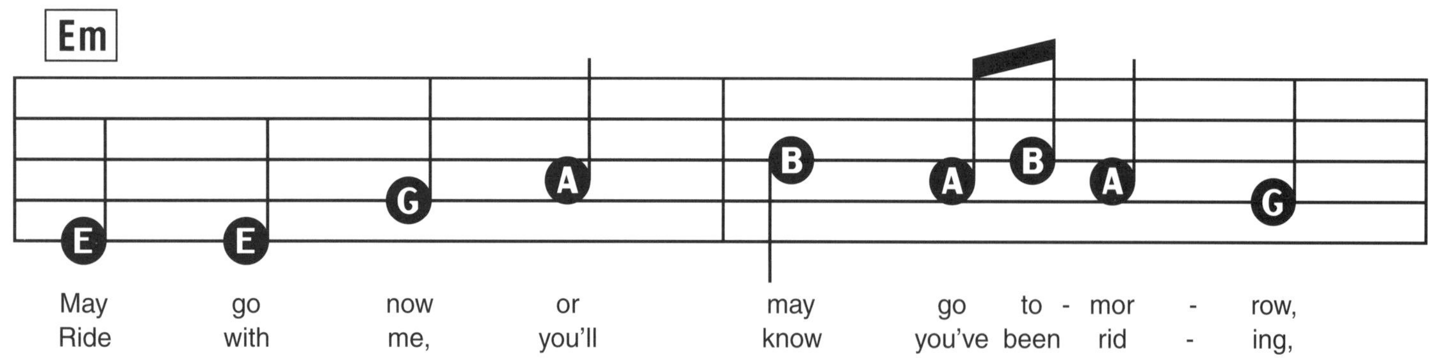
Em
E E G A B A B A G
May go now or may go to - mor - row,
Ride with me, you'll know you've been rid - ing,

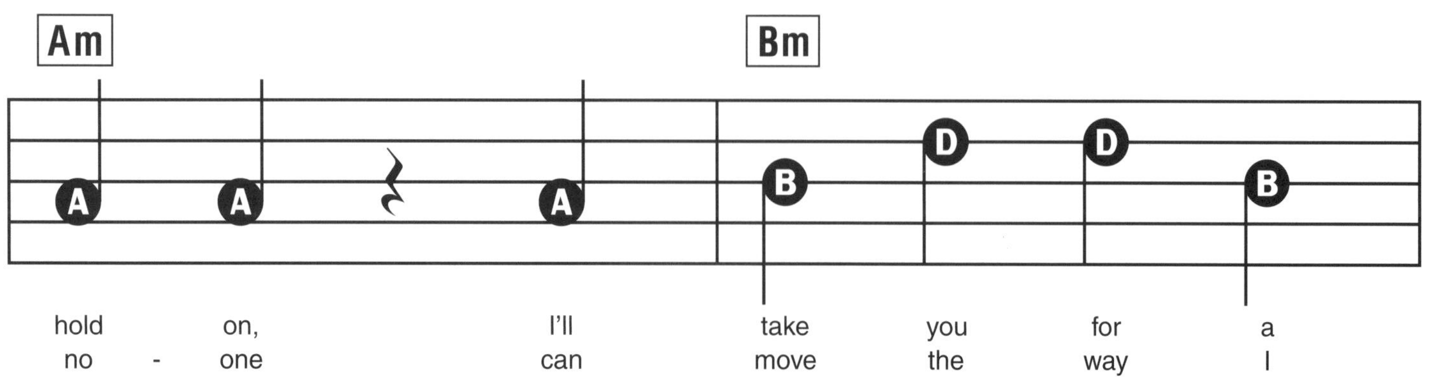
Am Bm
A A A B D D B
hold on, I'll take you for a
no - one can move the way I

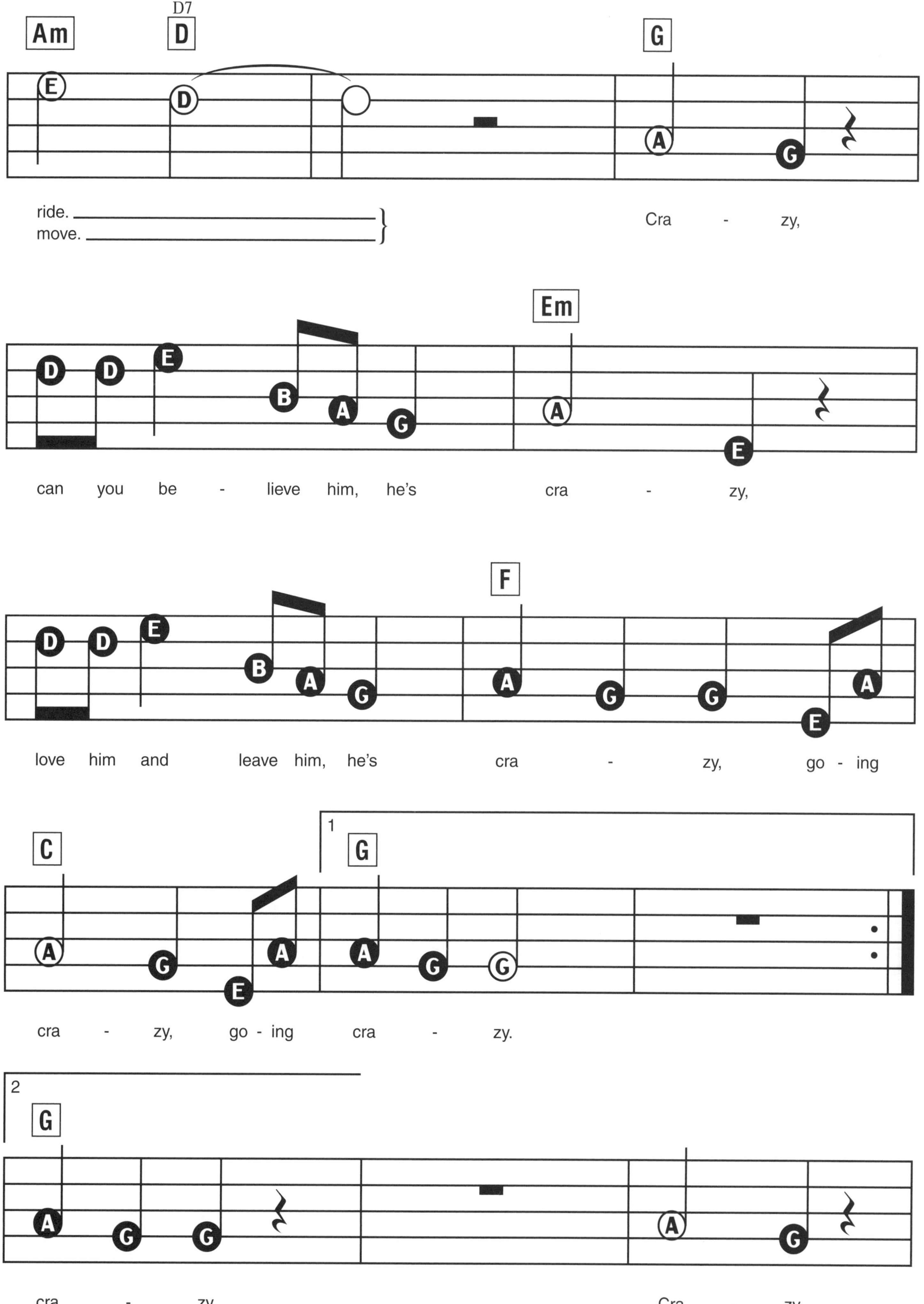
Am
D7
D
G
ride.
move.
Cra - zy,
Em
can you be - lieve him, he's cra - zy,
F
love him and leave him, he's cra - zy, go - ing
C
1
G
cra - zy, go - ing cra - zy.
2
G
cra - zy.
Cra - zy,

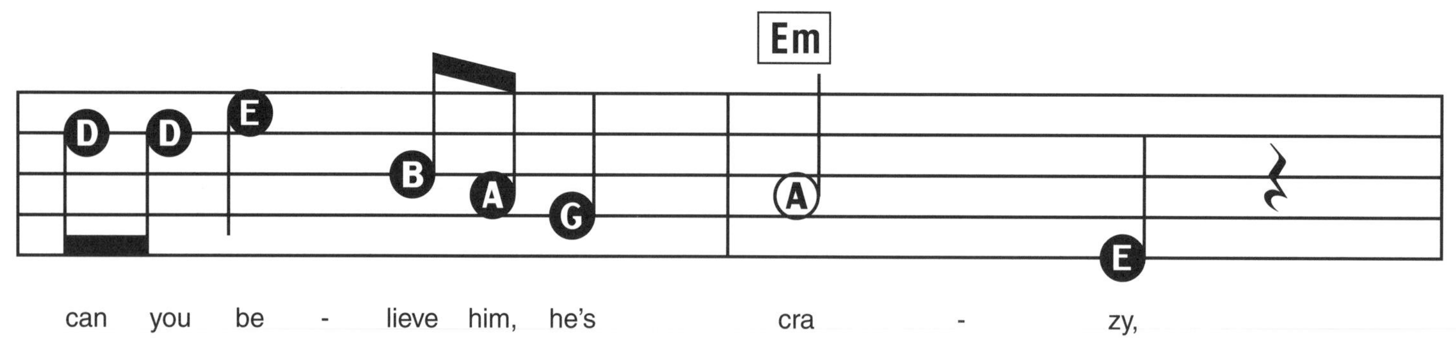
Em
D
D
E
B
A
G
A
E
can you be - lieve him, he's cra - zy,

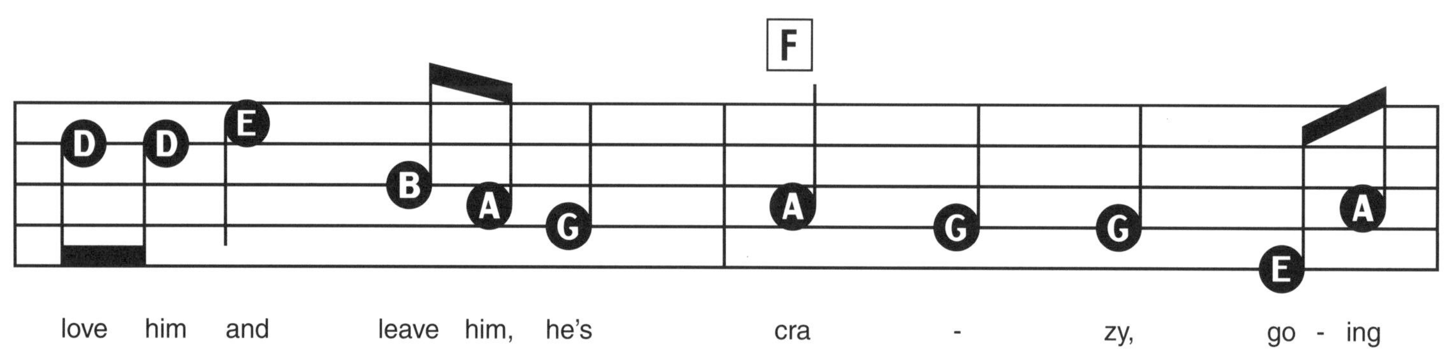
F
D
D
E
B
A
G
A
G
G
E
A
love him and leave him, he's cra - zy, go - ing

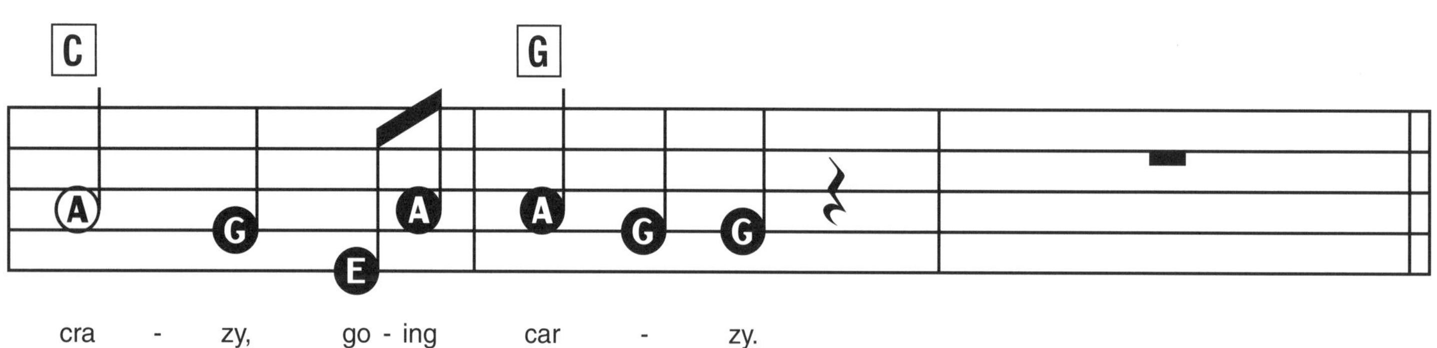
C
G
A
G
E
A
A
G
G
cra - zy, go - ing car - zy.

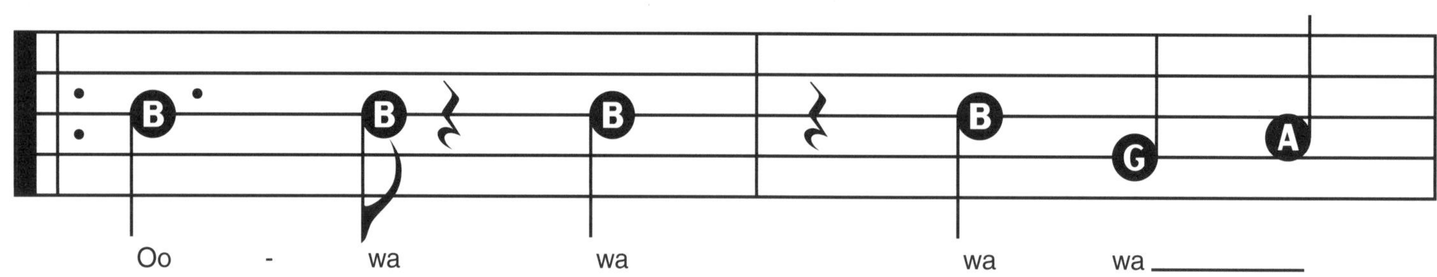
B
B
B
B
G
A
Oo - wa wa wa wa

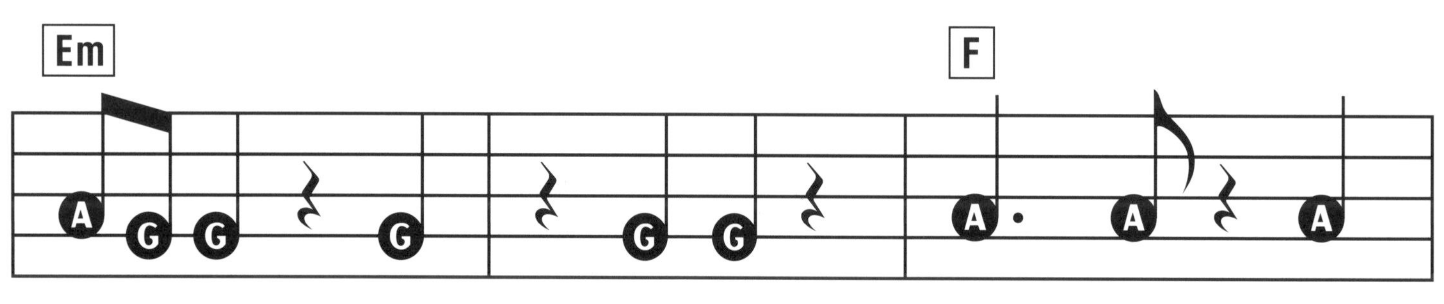
Em
F
A
G
G
G
G
G
A
A
A
oo - wa wa wa wa oo - wa wa

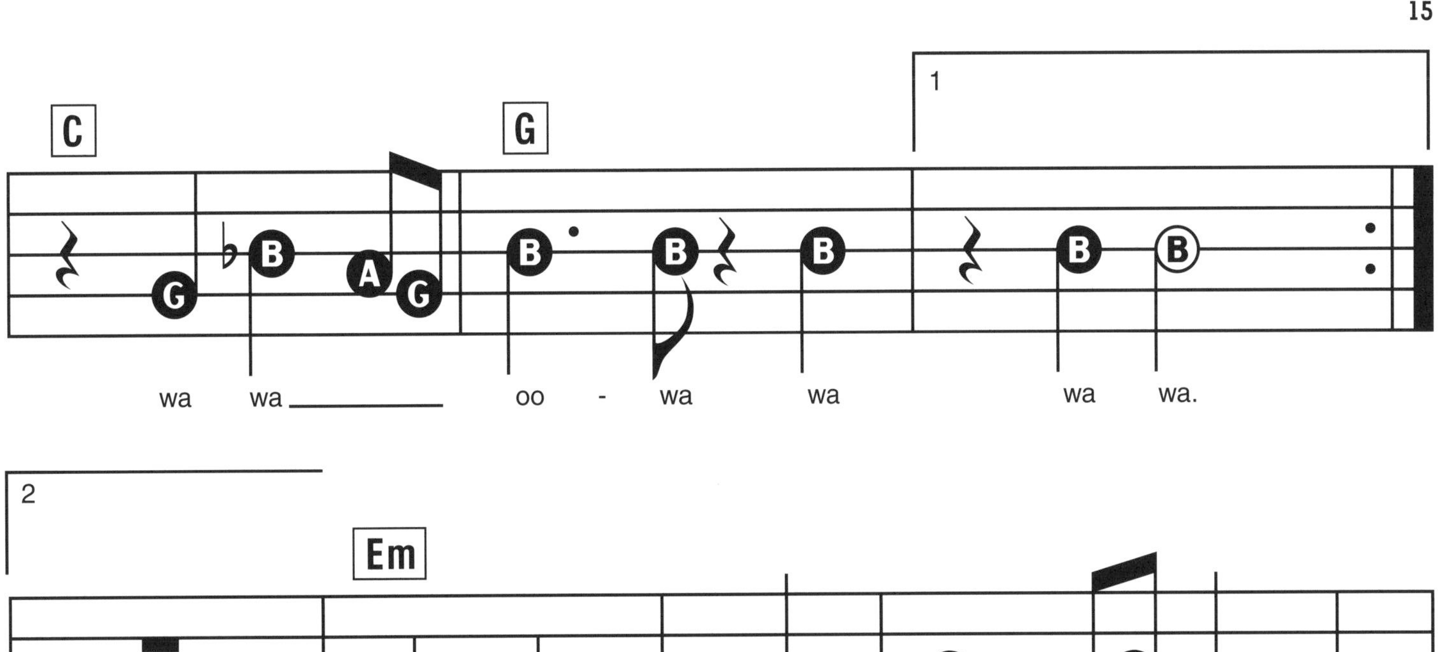
C
G
1
G B A G
B B B
B B
wa wa
oo - wa wa
wa wa.
2
Em
E E G A
B A B A G
Hold on tight, I'll
turn up the pres - sure;

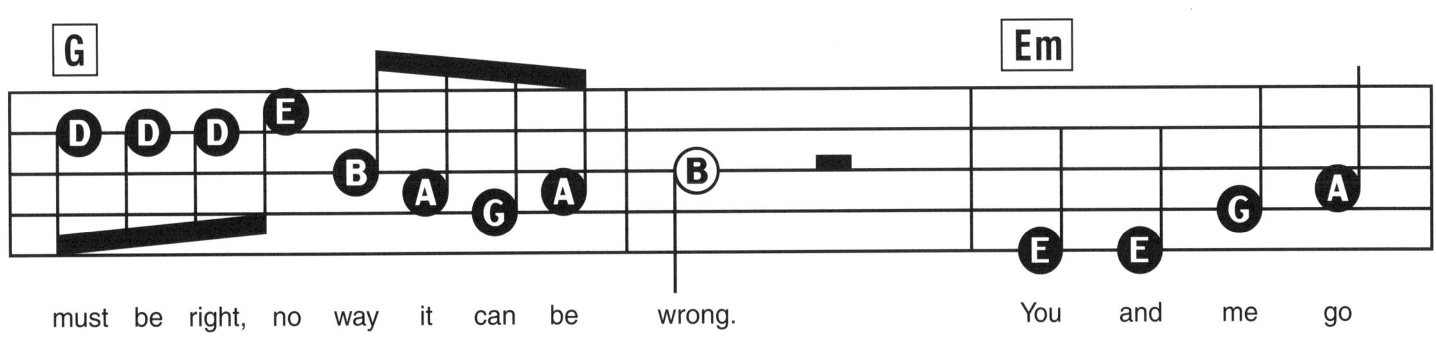
G
D D D E B A G A
B
Em
E E G A
must be right, no way it can be
wrong.
You and me go

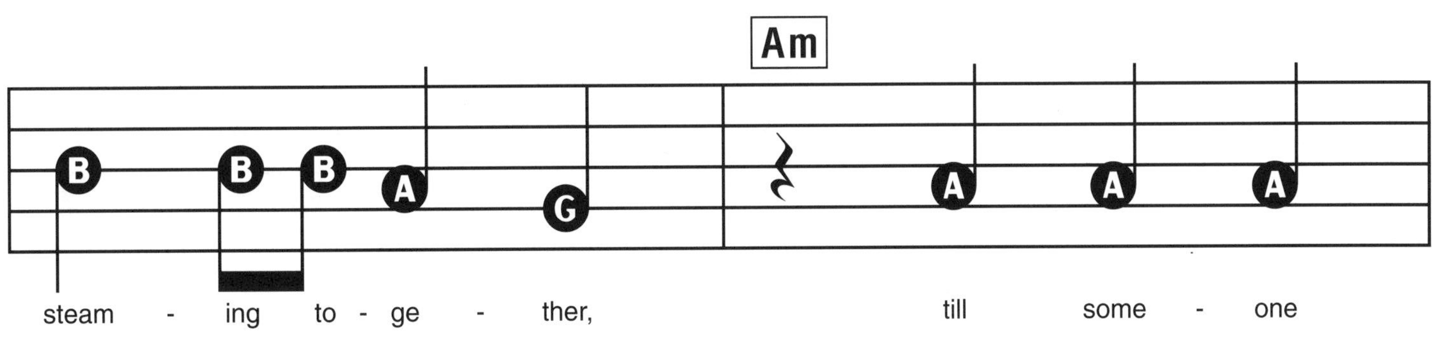
Am
B B B A G
A A A
steam - ing to - ge - ther,
till some - one

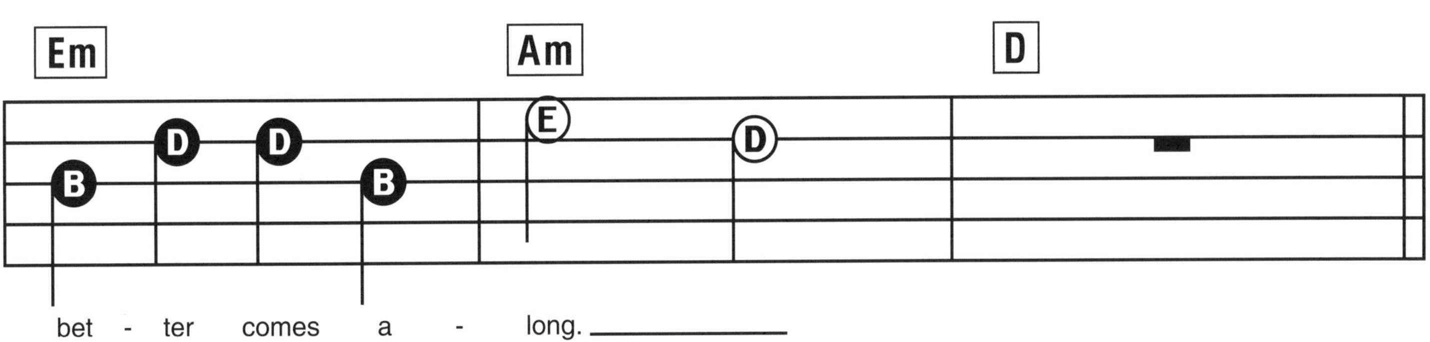
Em
Am
D
B D D B
E D
bet - ter comes a - long.

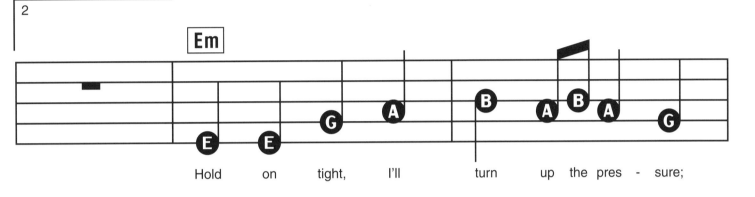

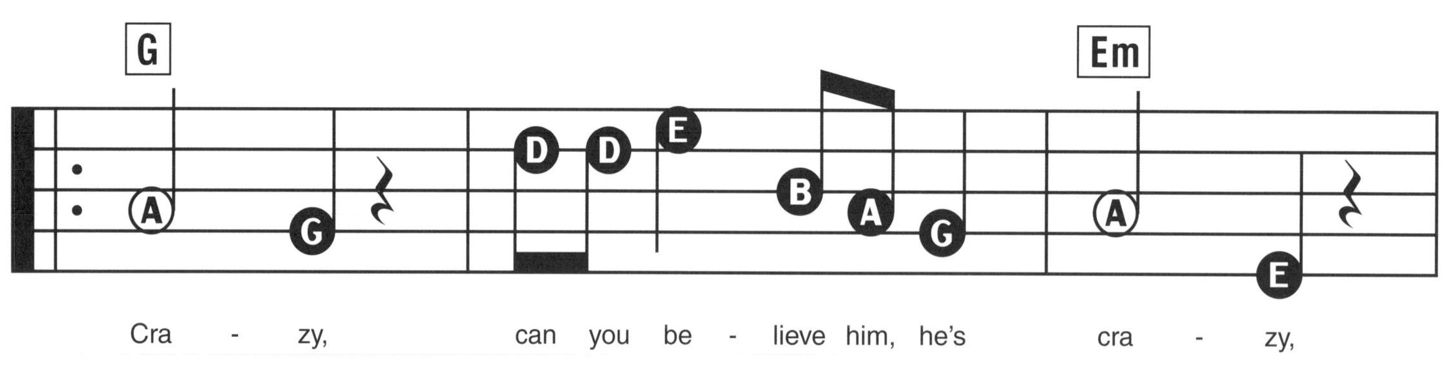

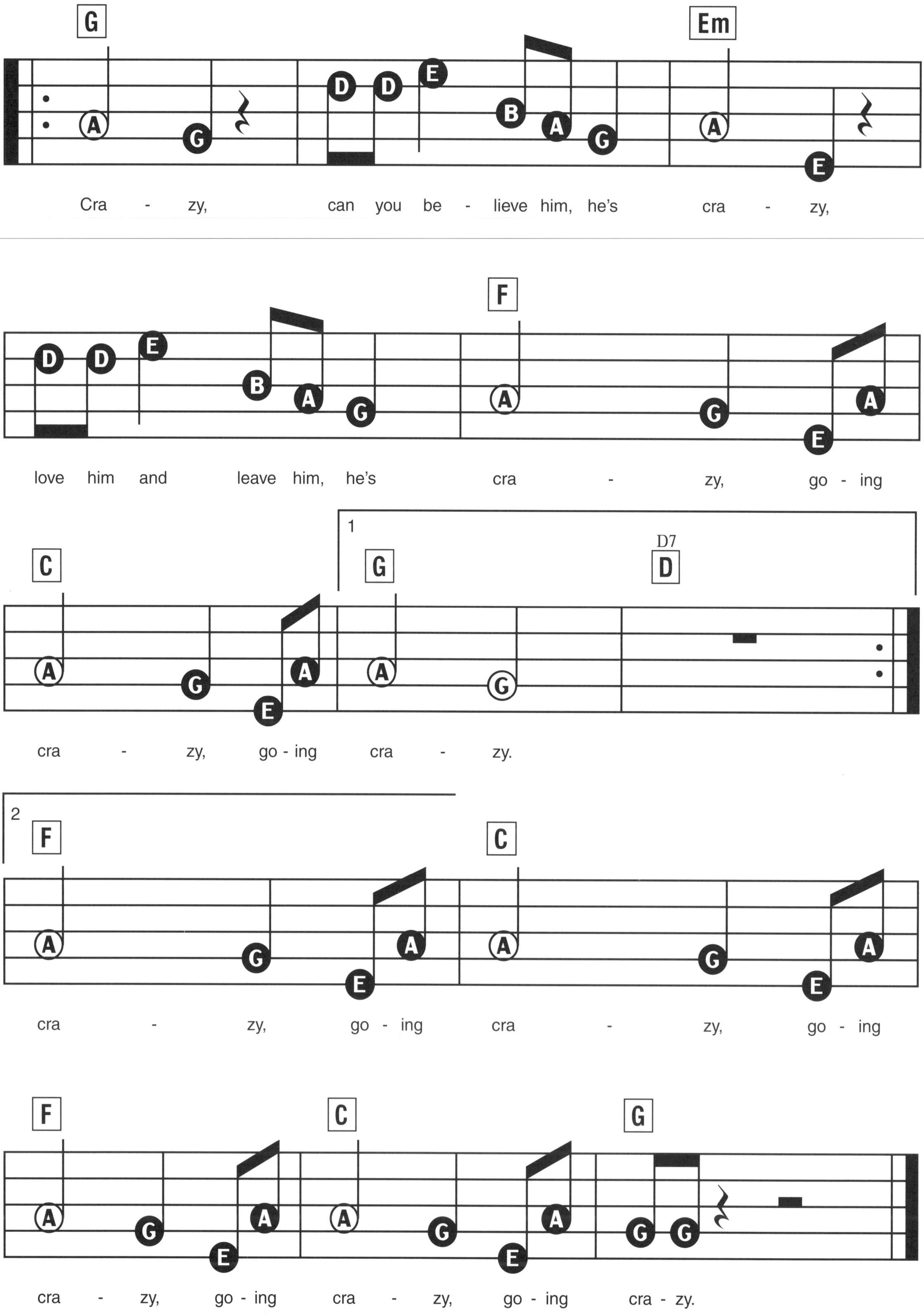

G
Em
Cra - zy, can you be - lieve him, he's cra - zy,
F
love him and leave him, he's cra - zy, go - ing
C
1
G
D7
D
cra - zy, go - ing cra - zy.
2
F
C
cra - zy, go - ing cra - zy, go - ing
F
C
G
cra - zy, go - ing cra - zy, go - ing cra - zy.

Make Up My Heart
from STARLIGHT EXPRESS

Music by Andrew Lloyd Webber
Lyrics by Richard Stilgoe

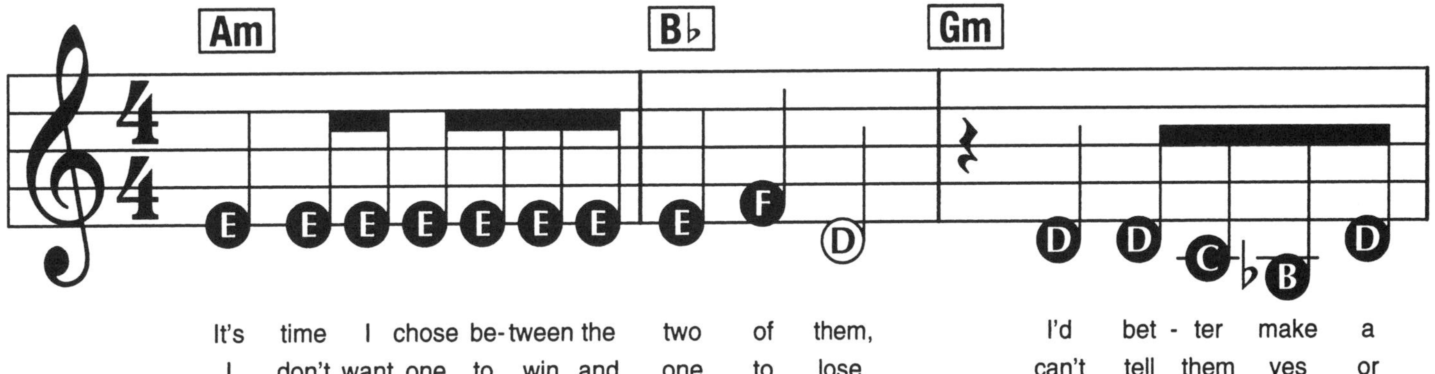

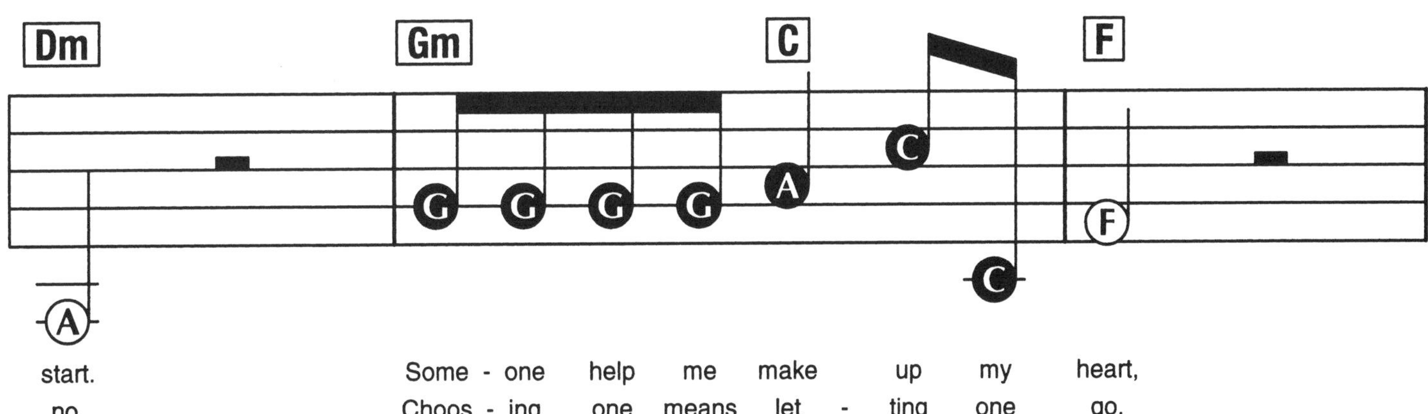

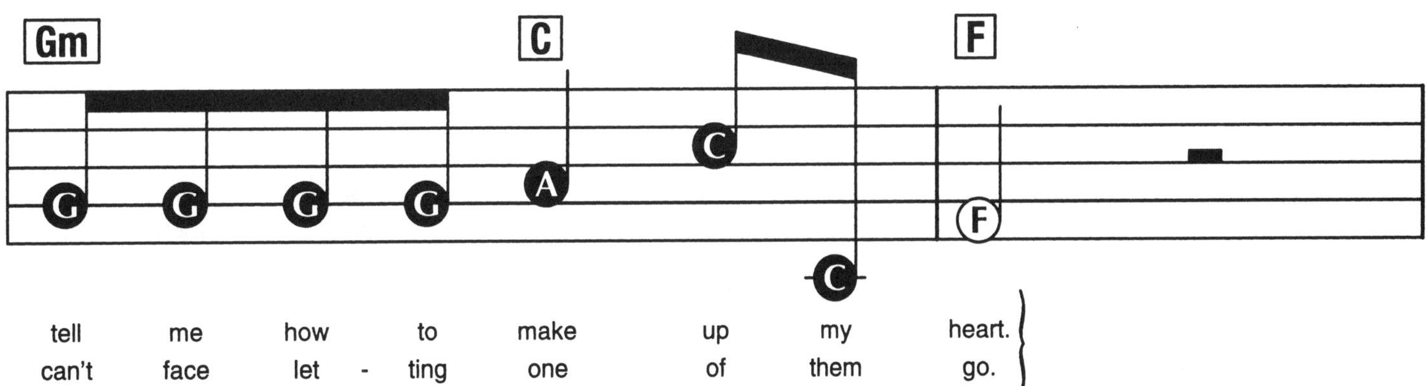

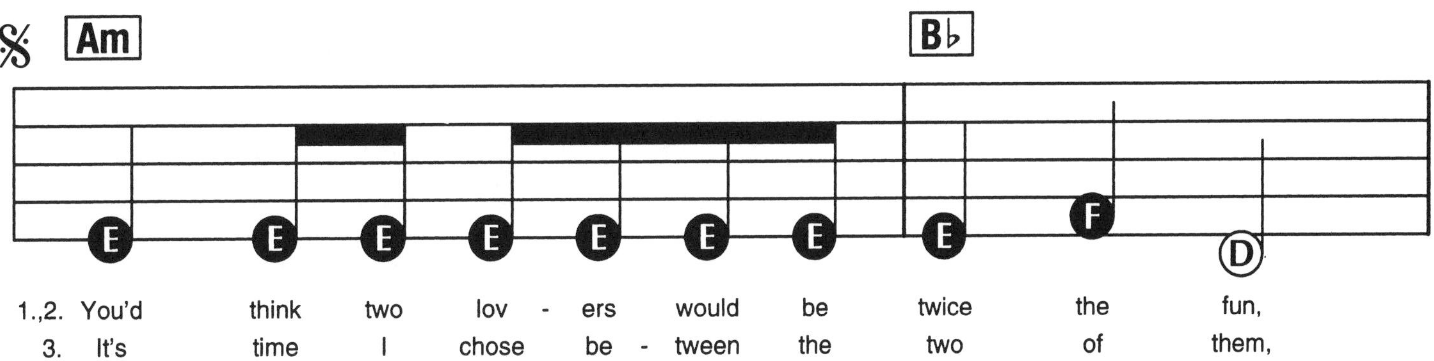

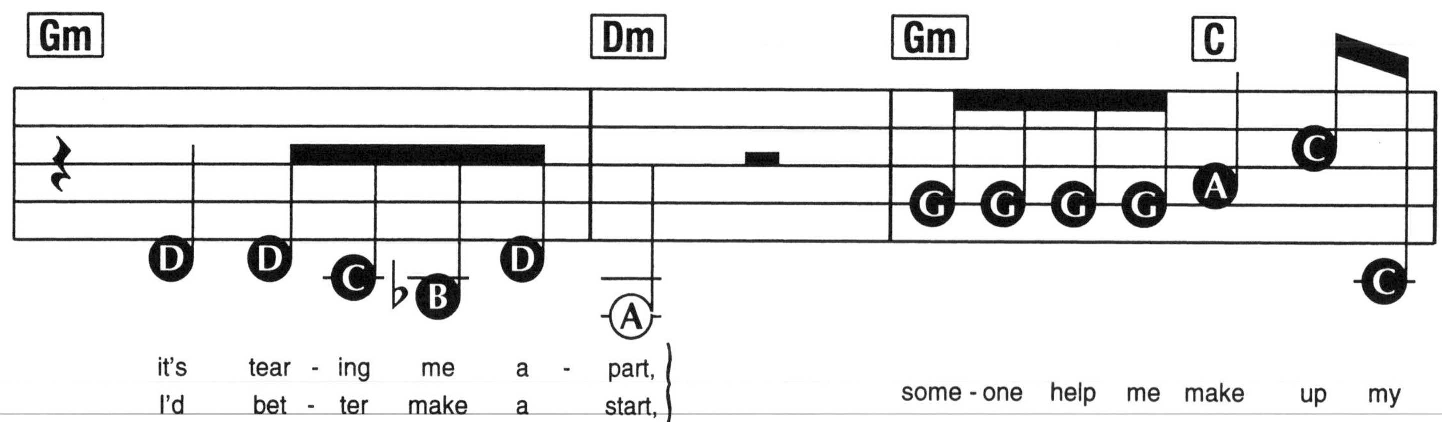
Gm
Dm
Gm
C
D D C B D A G G G G A C C
it's tear - ing me a - part,
I'd bet - ter make a start,
some - one help me make up my

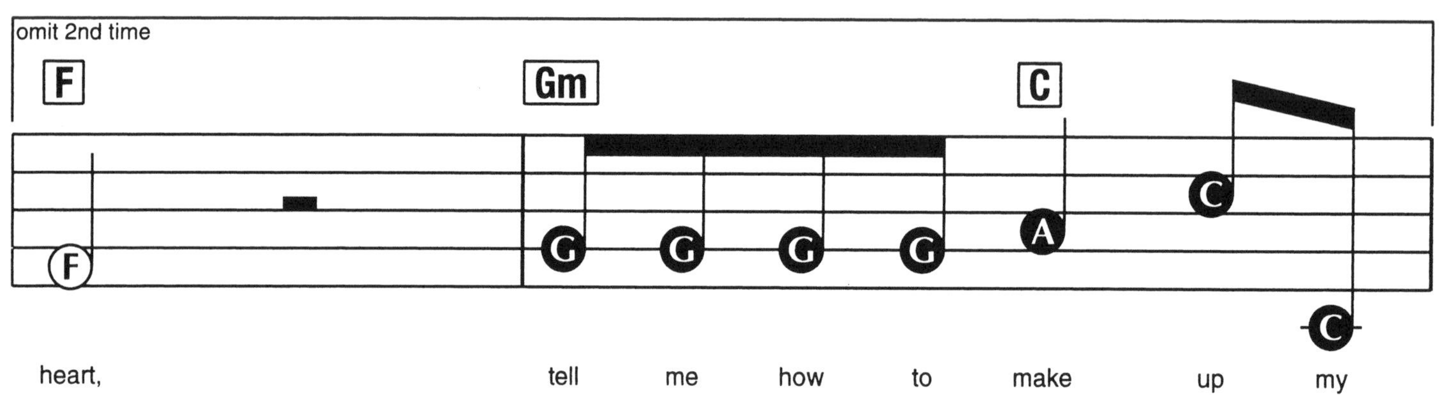
omit 2nd time
F
Gm
C
F G G G G A C C
heart,
tell me how to make up my

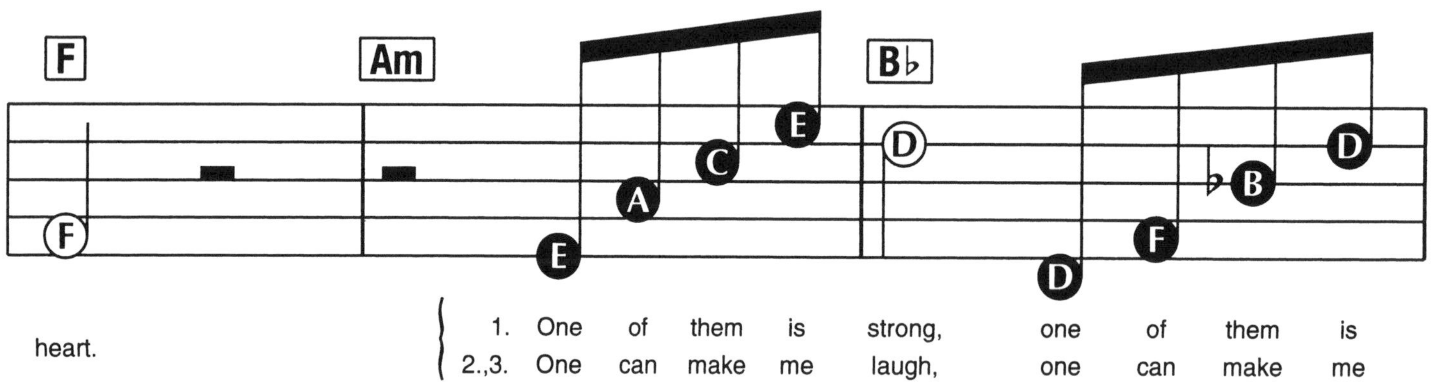
F
Am
B♭
F E A C E D D F B D
heart.
1. One of them is strong, one of them is
2.,3. One can make me laugh, one can make me

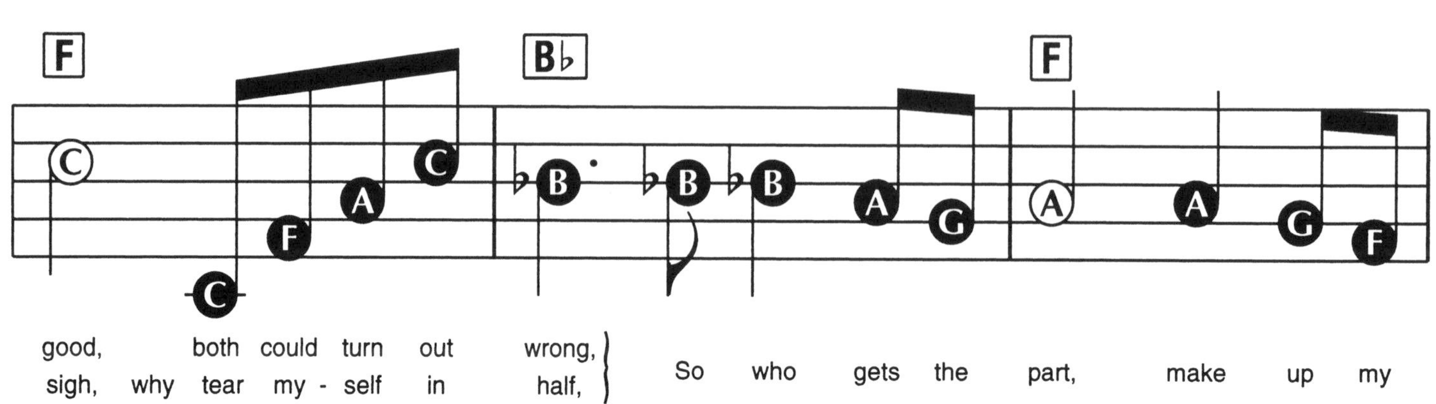
F
B♭
F
C C F A C B B B A G A A G F
good, both could turn out wrong,
sigh, why tear my - self in half,
So who gets the part, make up my

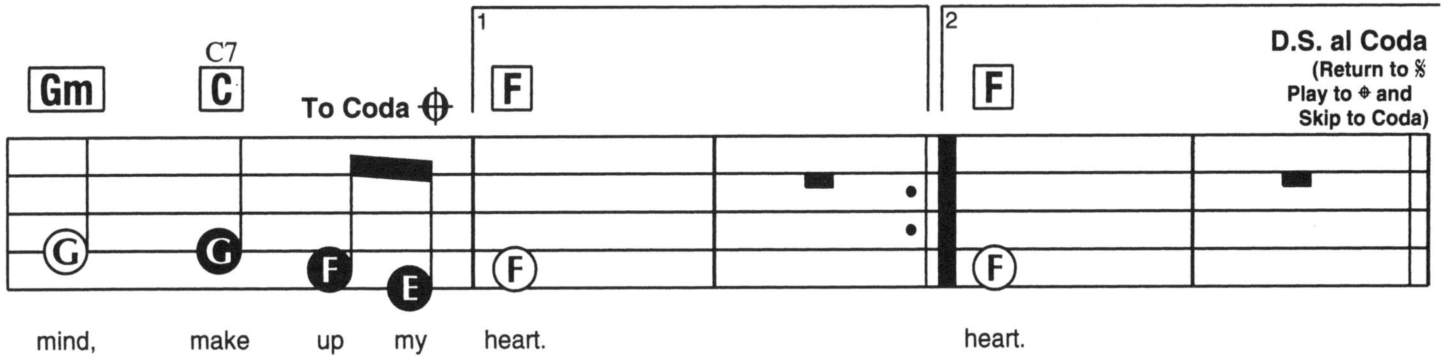
Gm
C7
C
To Coda
1
F
2
F
D.S. al Coda
(Return to 𝄋
Play to 𝄌 and
Skip to Coda)
mind, make up my heart.
heart.

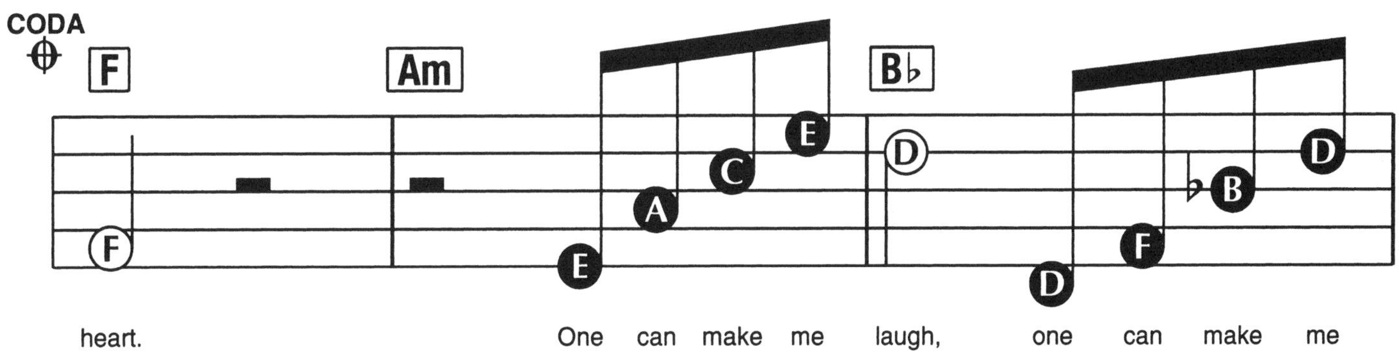
CODA
F
Am
B♭
heart.
One can make me laugh, one can make me

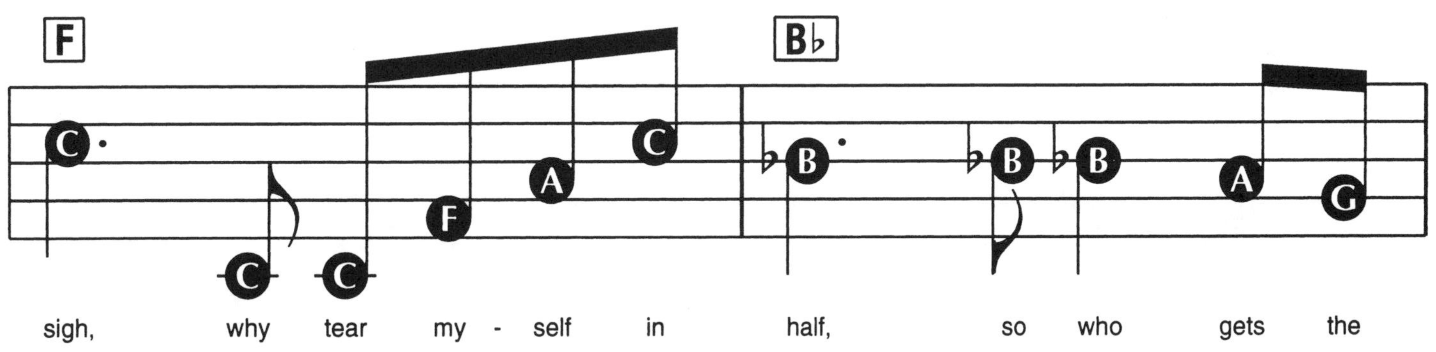
F
B♭
sigh, why tear my - self in half, so who gets the

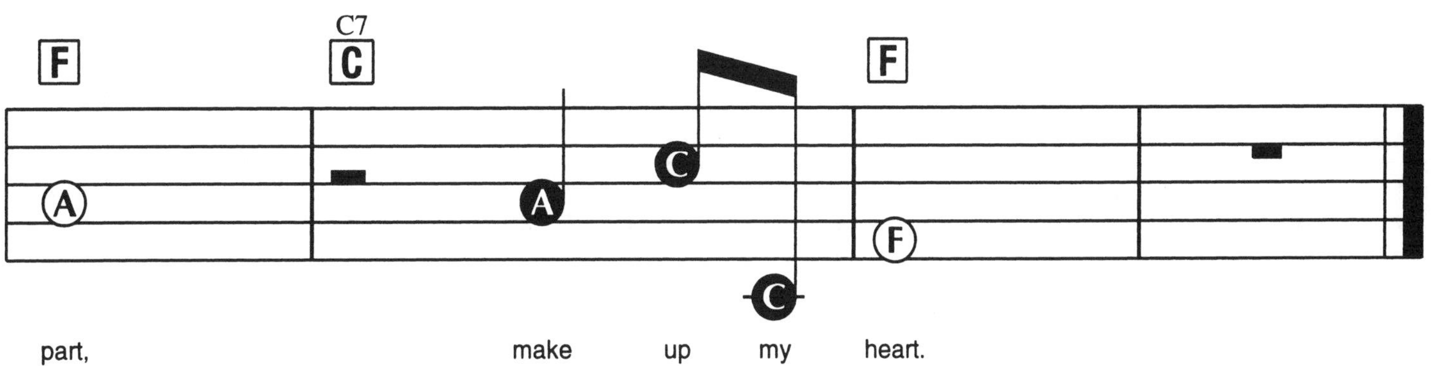
F
C7
C
F
part, make up my heart.

Everything's Alright

from JESUS CHRIST SUPERSTAR

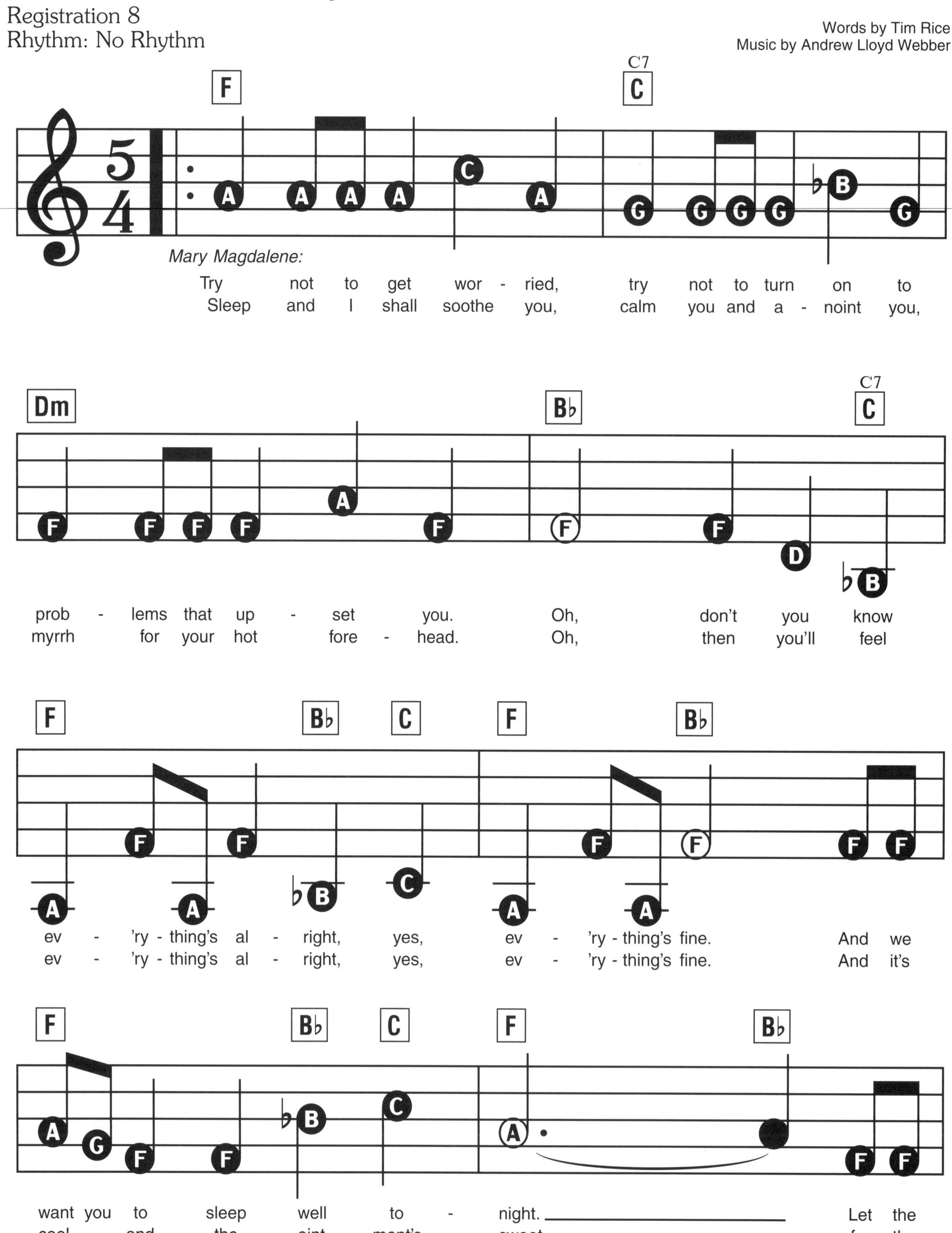

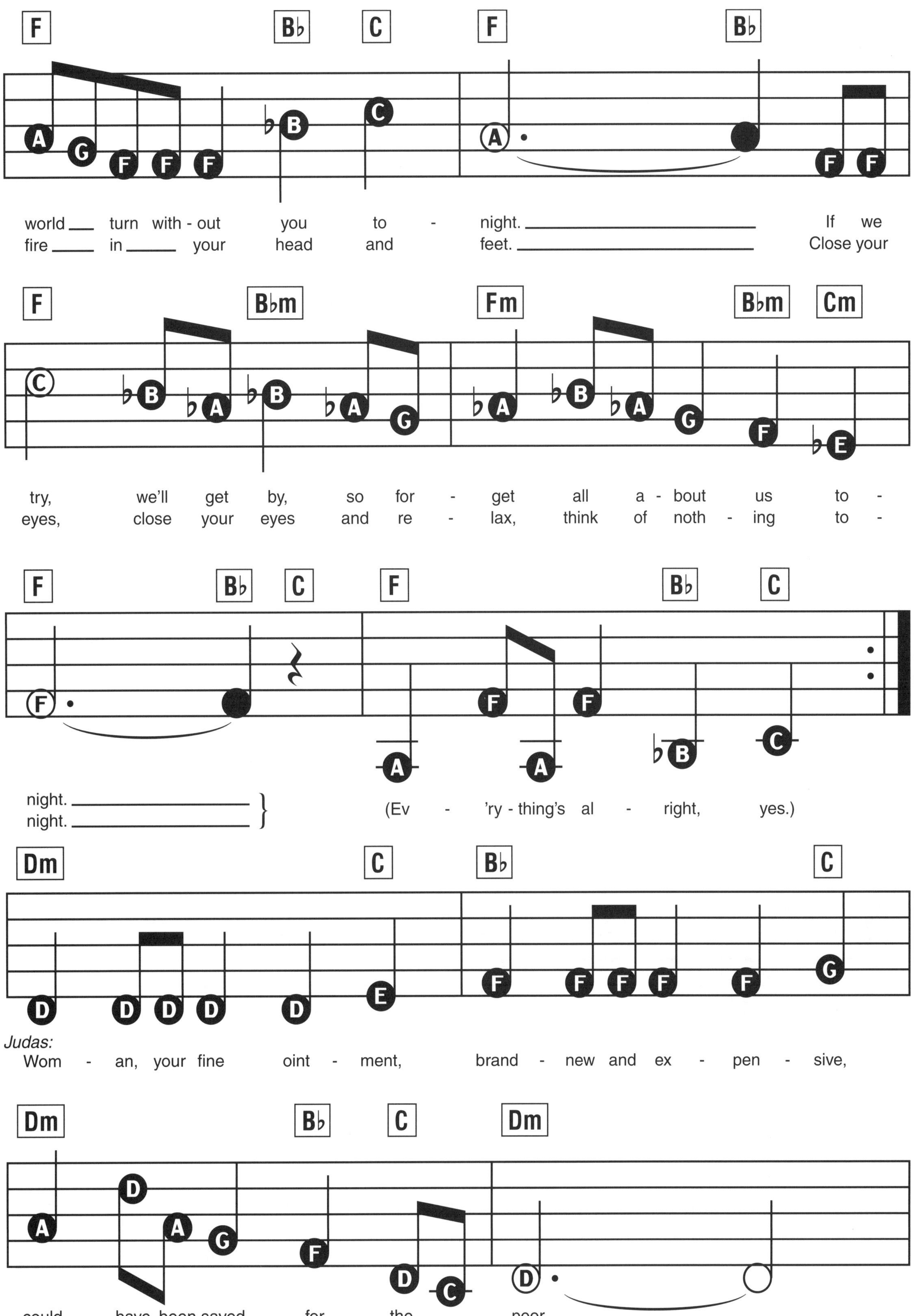
F Bb C F Bb
world ___ turn with - out you to - night. ___ If we
fire ___ in ___ your head and feet. ___ Close your
F Bbm Fm Bbm Cm
try, we'll get by, so for - get all a - bout us to -
eyes, close your eyes and re - lax, think of noth - ing to -
F Bb C F Bb C
night. ___
night. ___
(Ev - 'ry - thing's al - right, yes.)
Dm C Bb C
Judas:
Wom - an, your fine oint - ment, brand - new and ex - pen - sive,
Dm Bb C Dm
could have been saved for the ___ poor. ___

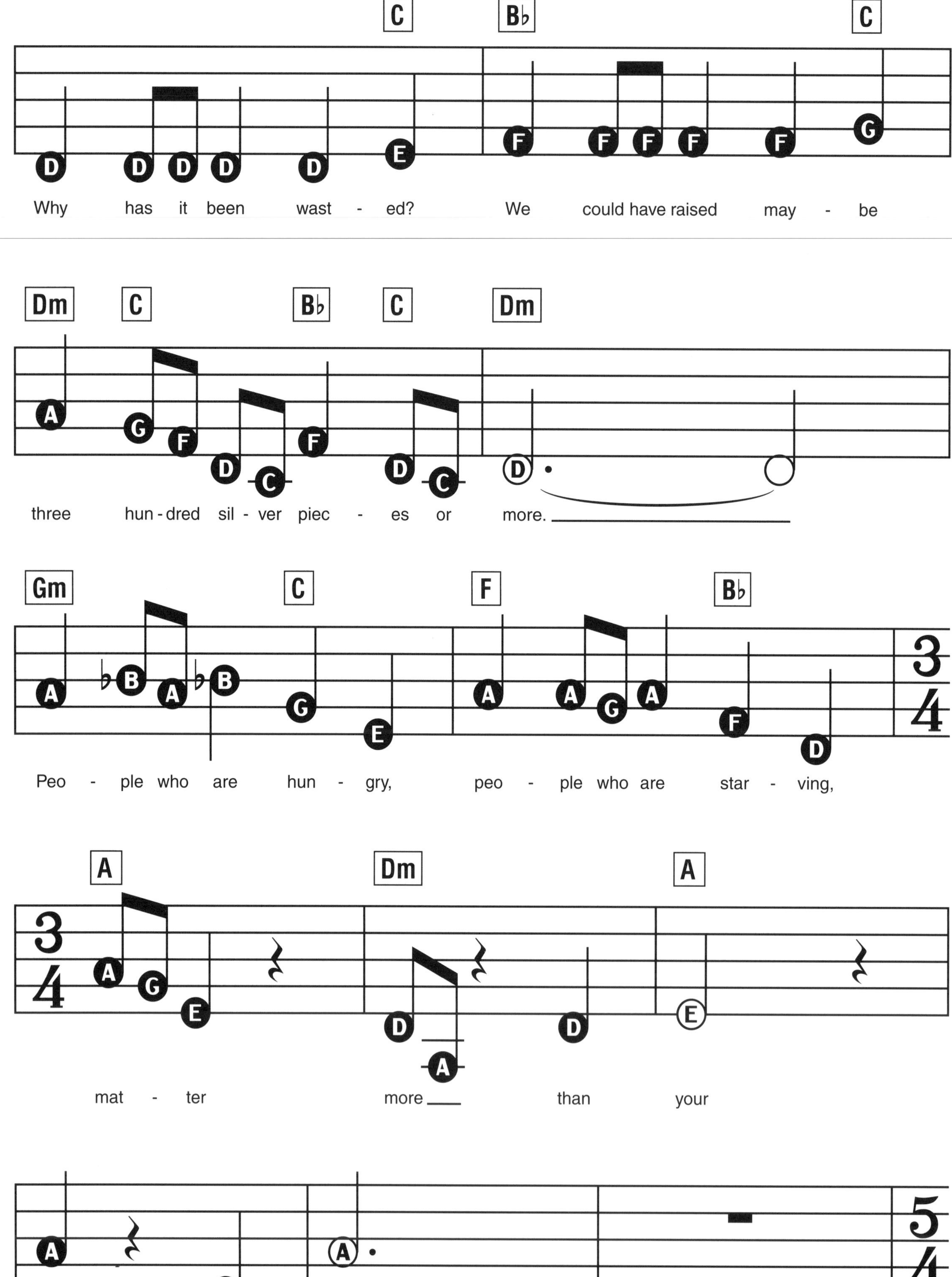
C Bb C
D D D D D E F F F F F G
Why has it been wast - ed? We could have raised may - be
Dm C Bb C Dm
A G F D C F D C D
three hun - dred sil - ver piec - es or more.
Gm C F Bb
A B A B G E A A G A F D
Peo - ple who are hun - gry, peo - ple who are star - ving,
A Dm A
A G E D A D E
mat - ter more than your
A E A
feet and hair.

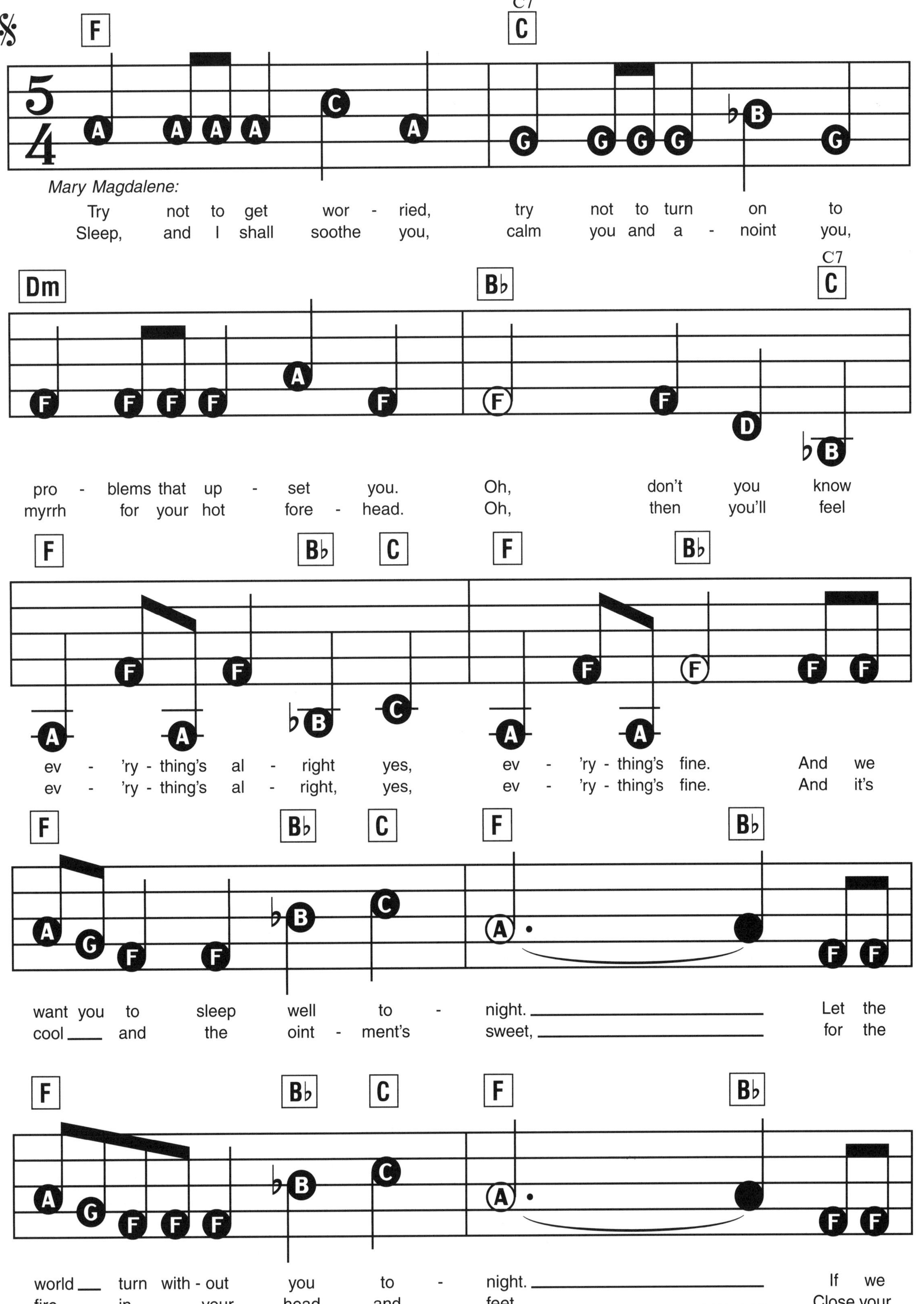
F C7 C
5/4
Mary Magdalene:
Try not to get wor - ried, try not to turn on to
Sleep, and I shall soothe you, calm you and a - noint you,
Dm B♭ C7 C
pro - blems that up - set you. Oh, don't you know
myrrh for your hot fore - head. Oh, then you'll feel
F B♭ C F B♭
ev - 'ry - thing's al - right yes, ev - 'ry - thing's fine. And we
ev - 'ry - thing's al - right, yes, ev - 'ry - thing's fine. And it's
F B♭ C F B♭
want you to sleep well to - night. Let the
cool and the oint - ment's sweet, for the
F B♭ C F B♭
world turn with - out you to - night. If we
fire in your head and feet. Close your

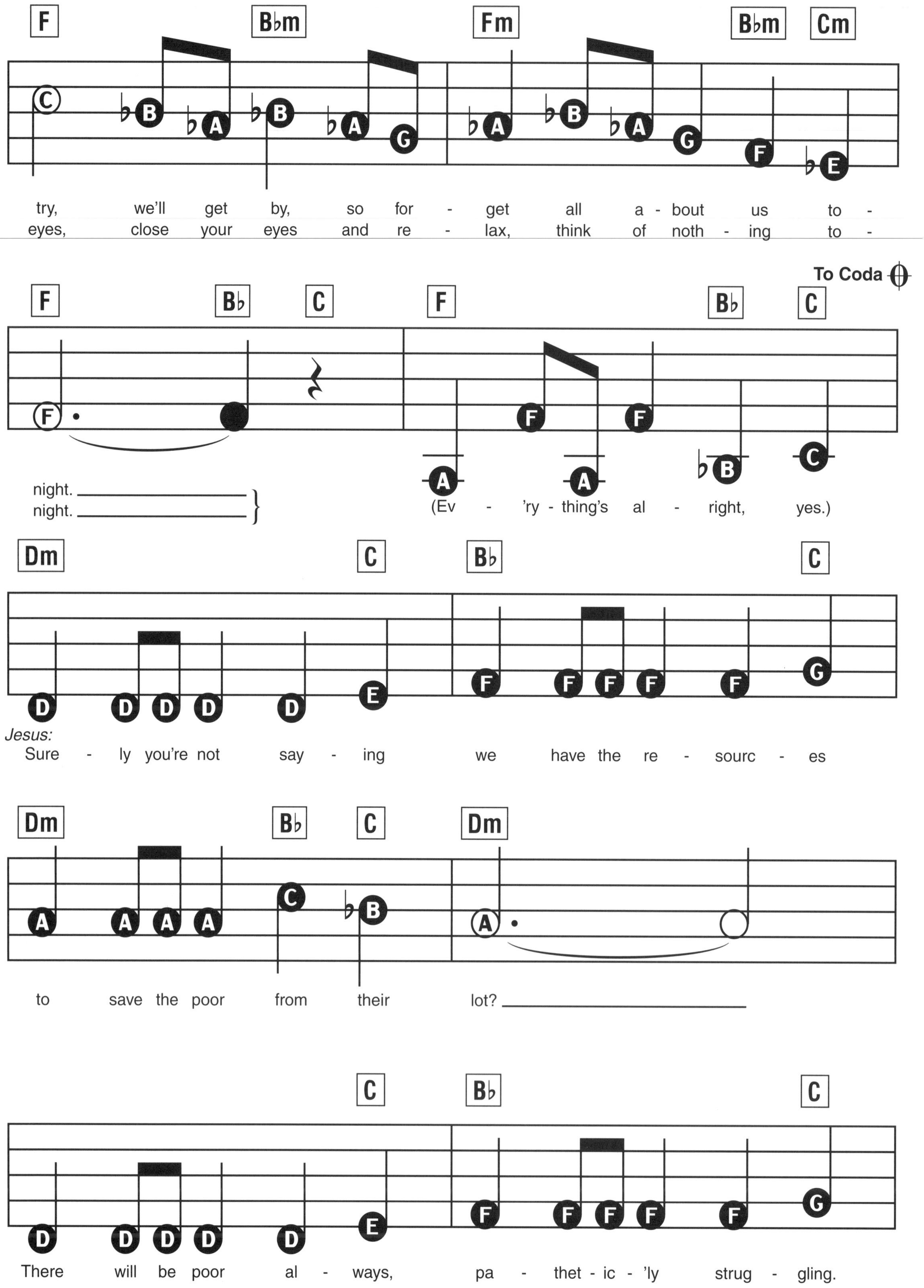

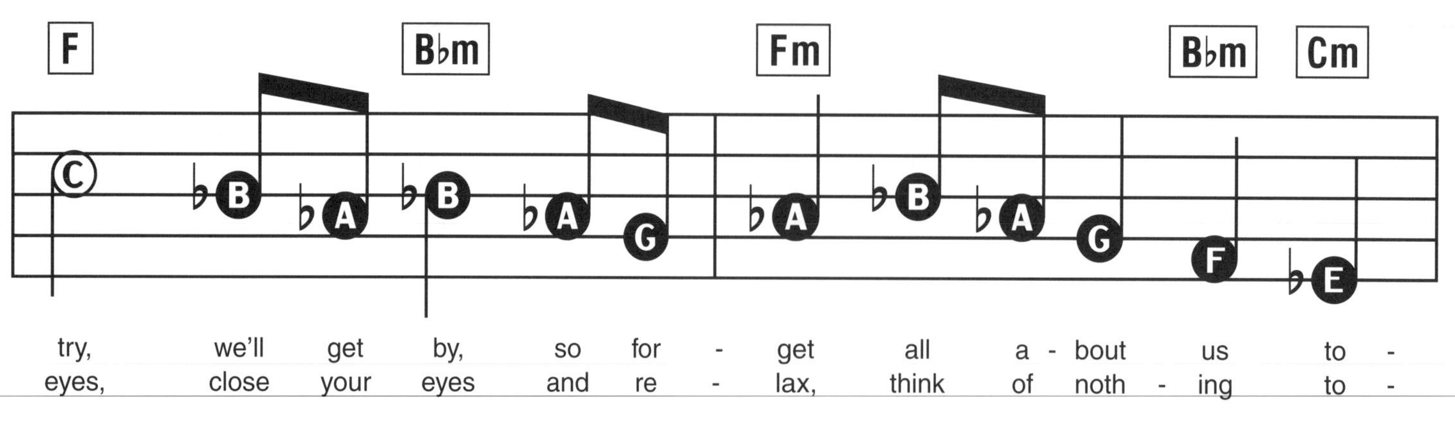

To Coda

F B♭ C F B♭ C

F A F F A B♭ C

night. ______
night. ______

(Ev - 'ry - thing's al - right, yes.)

Dm C B♭ C

D D D D D E F F F F F G

Jesus:
Sure - ly you're not say - ing we have the re - sourc - es

Dm B♭ C Dm

A A A A C B♭ A

to save the poor from their lot? ______

C B♭ C

D D D D D E F F F F F G

There will be poor al - ways, pa - thet - ic - 'ly strug - gling.

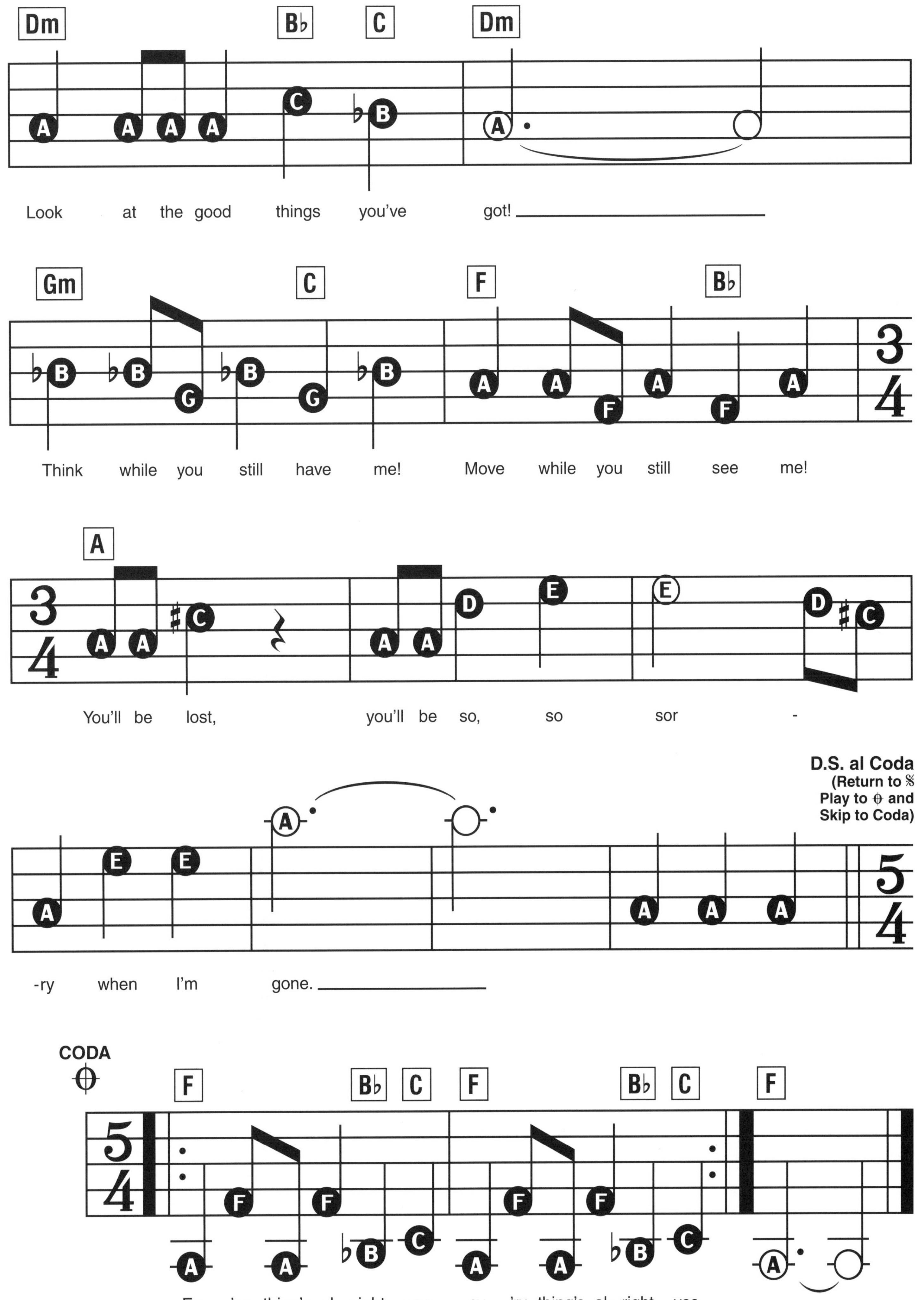
Dm
B♭
C
Dm
Look at the good things you've got!
Gm
C
F
B♭
Think while you still have me! Move while you still see me!
A
You'll be lost, you'll be so, so sor - -ry when I'm gone.
D.S. al Coda
(Return to 𝄋
Play to ⊕ and
Skip to Coda)
CODA
F
B♭
C
F
B♭
C
F
Ev - 'ry - thing's al - right, yes, ev - 'ry - thing's al - right, yes.

The First Man You Remember

from ASPECTS OF LOVE

Registration 1
Rhythm: Fox Trot or Swing

Music by Andrew Lloyd Webber
Lyrics by Don Black and Charles Hart

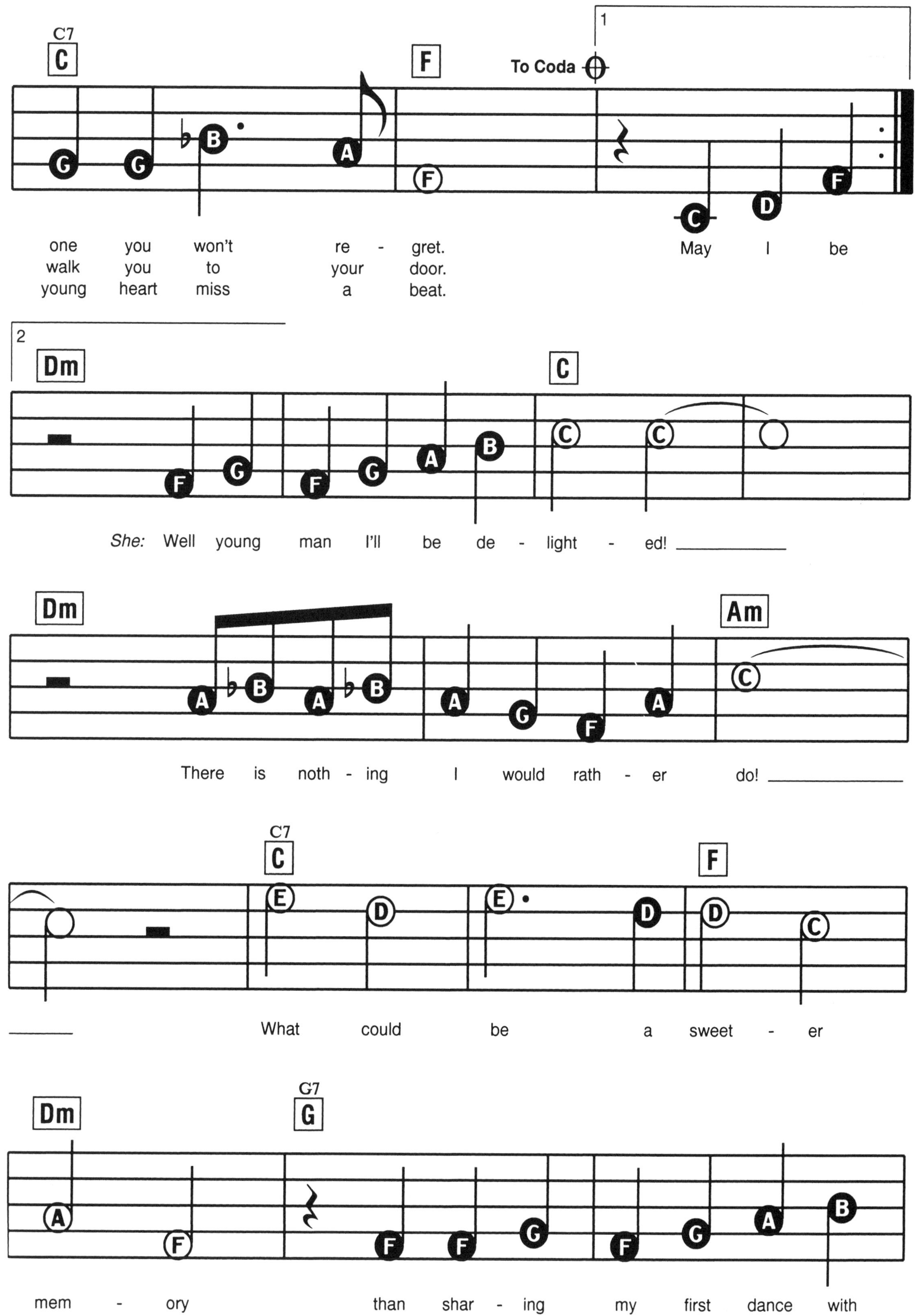
C7
C
F
To Coda
1
one you won't re - gret.
walk you to your door.
young heart miss a beat.
May I be
2
Dm
C
She: Well young man I'll be de - light - ed!
Dm
Am
There is noth - ing I would rath - er do!
C7
C
F
What could be a sweet - er
Dm
G7
G
mem - ory than shar - ing my first dance with

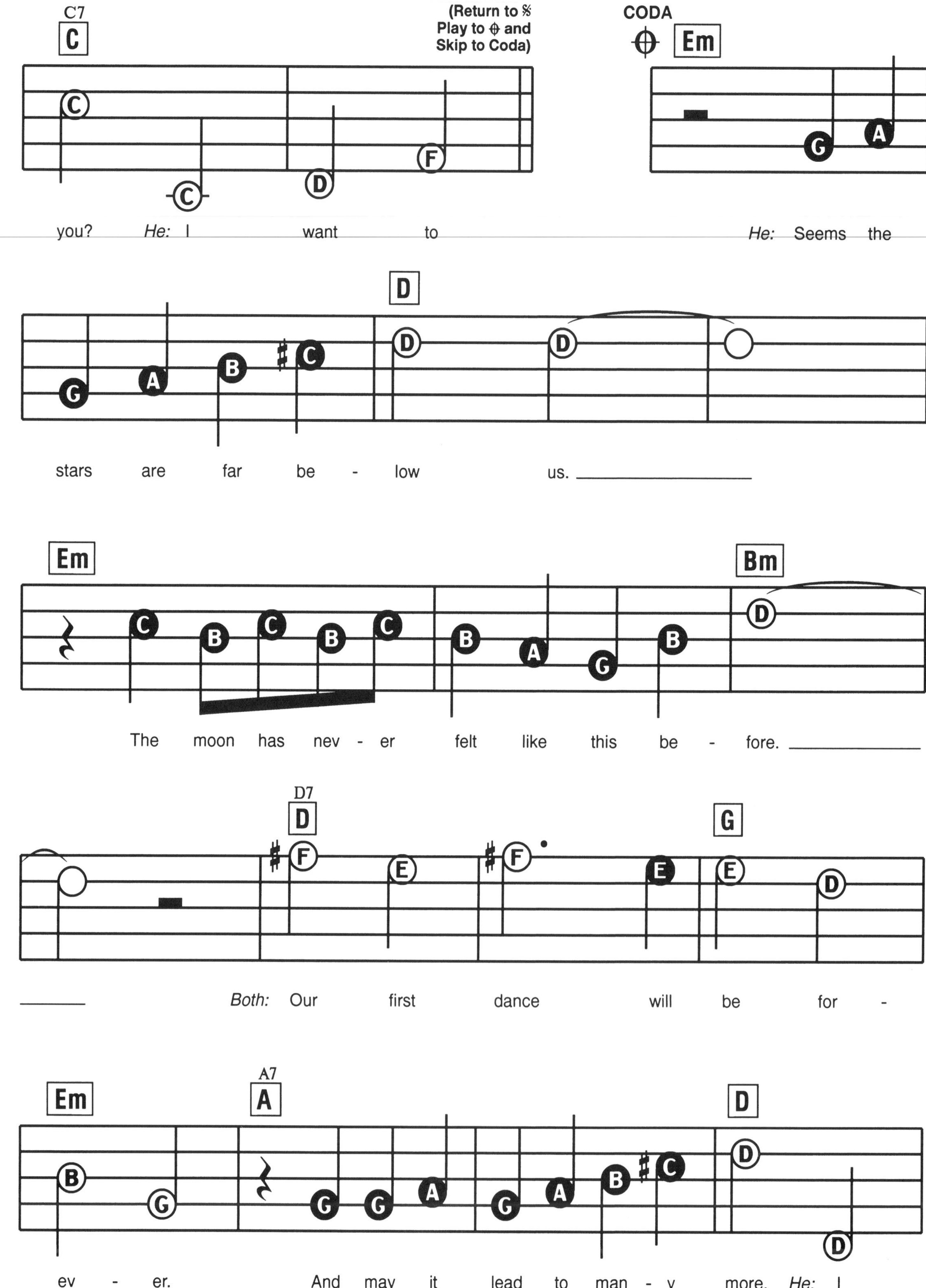

D.S. al Coda
(Return to 𝄋
Play to ⊕ and
Skip to Coda)
CODA
C7
C
Em
D
Bm
D7
G
A7
A
you? He: I want to
He: Seems the
stars are far be - low us.
The moon has nev - er felt like this be - fore.
Both: Our first dance will be for -
ev - er. And may it lead to man - y more. He: I

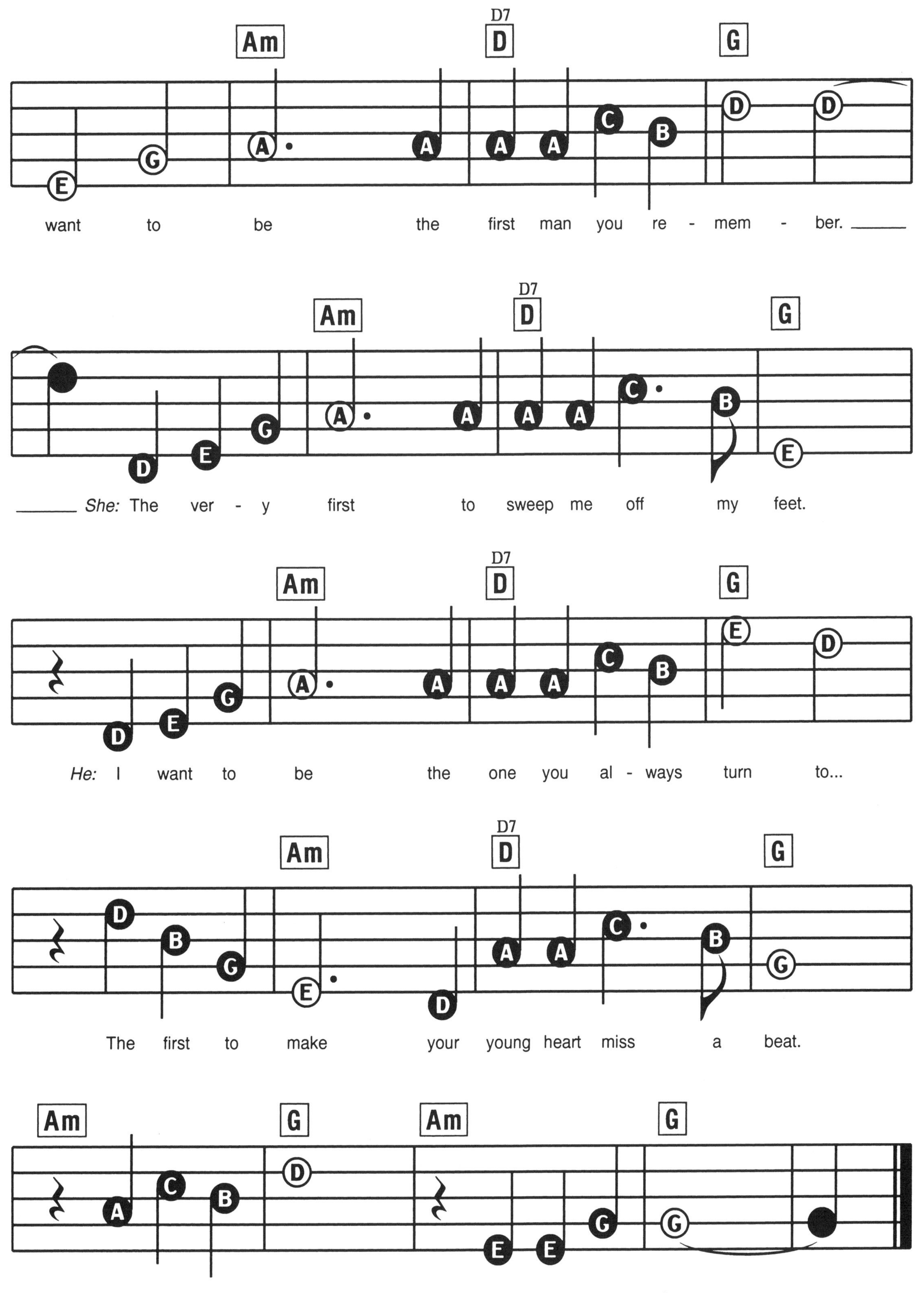
Am
D7
D
G
want to be the first man you re - mem - ber.
She: The ver - y first to sweep me off my feet.
He: I want to be the one you al - ways turn to...
The first to make your young heart miss a beat.
She: The ver - y first...
Both: The ver - y first...

Gus: The Theatre Cat

from CATS

Registration 9
Rhythm: Waltz

Music by Andrew Lloyd Webber
Text by T.S. Eliot

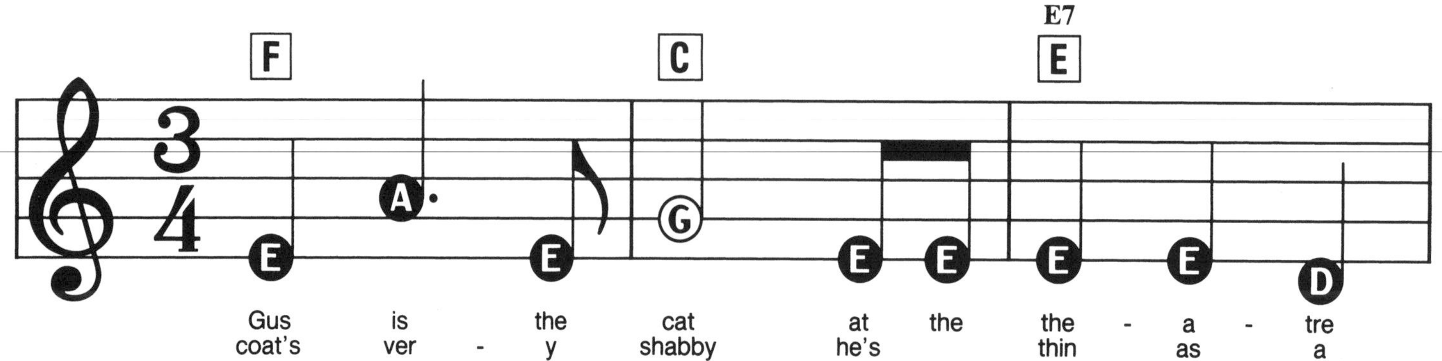

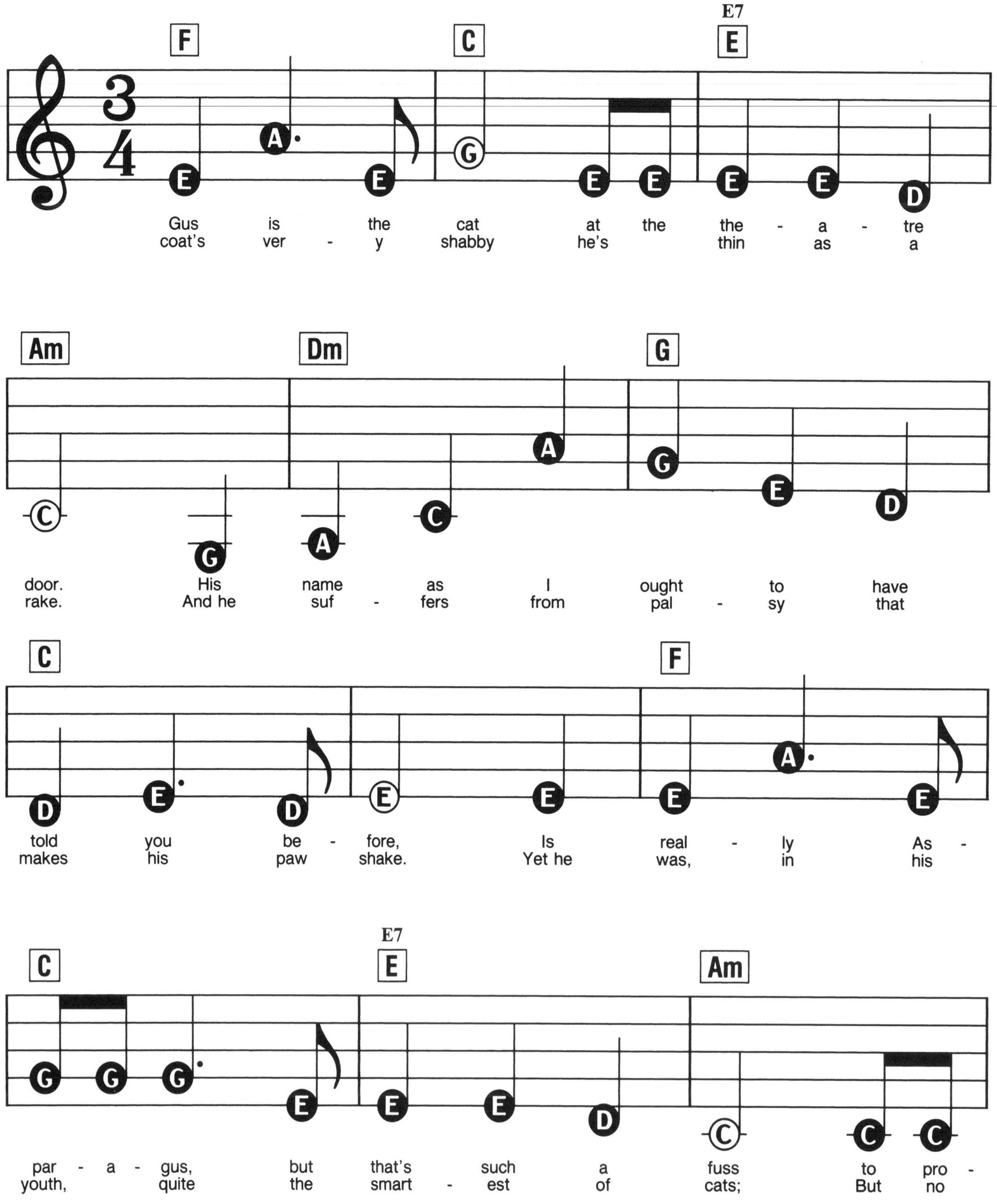

Am Dm G
C G A C A G E D
door. His name as I ought to have
rake. And he suf - fers from pal - sy that

C F
D E D E E E A E
told you be - fore, Is real - ly As -
makes his paw shake. Yet he was, in his

C E7 E Am
G G G E E E D C C C
par - a - gus, but that's such a fuss to pro -
youth, quite the smart - est of cats; But no

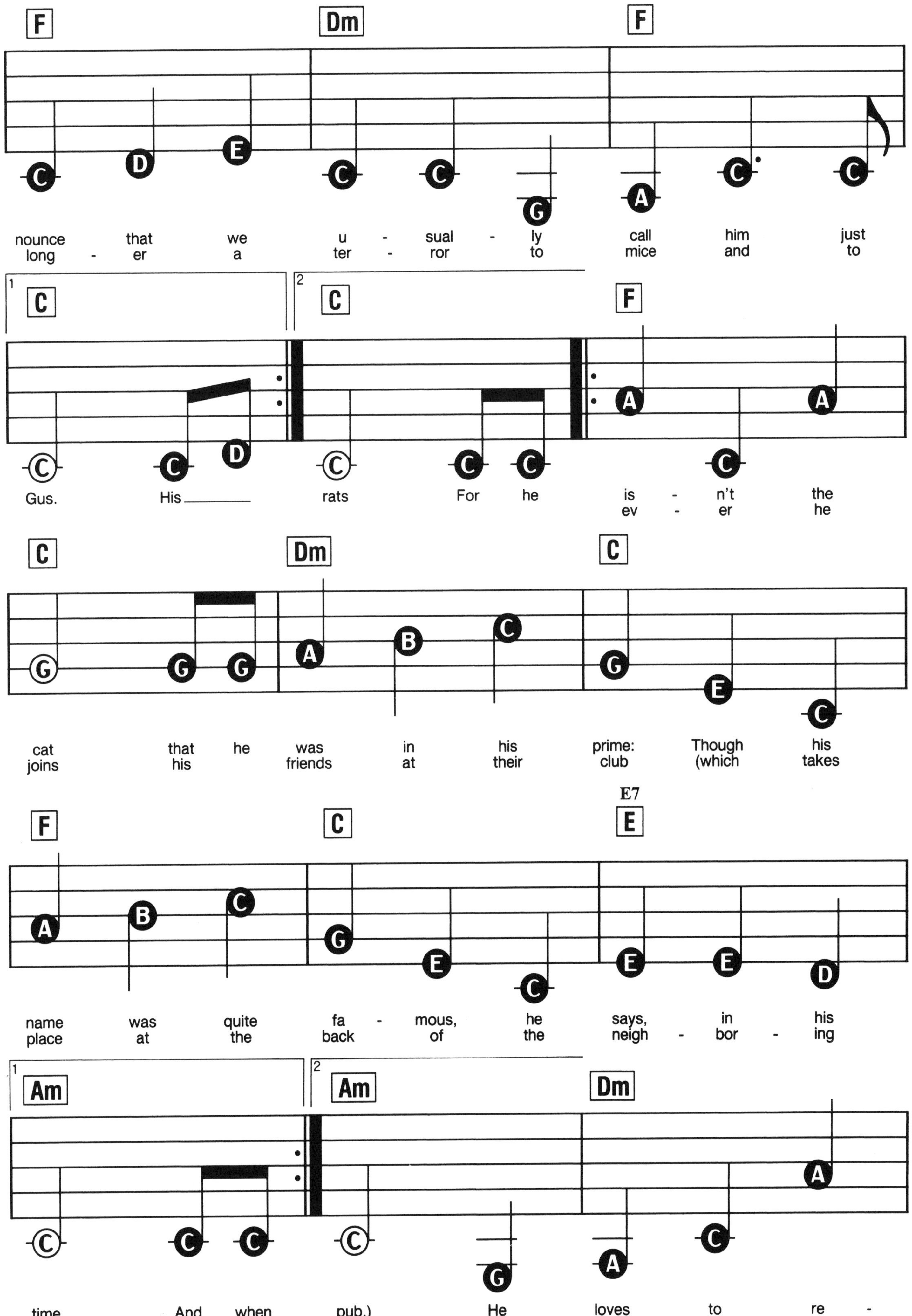
F
Dm
F
nounce that we u - sual - ly call him just
long - er a ter - ror to mice and to
1
C
2
C
F
Gus. His
rats For he is - n't the
ev - er he
C
Dm
C
cat that he was in his prime: Though his
joins his friends at their club (which takes
F
C
E7
E
name was quite fa - mous, he says, in his
place at the back of the neigh - bor - ing
1
Am
2
Am
Dm
time And when
pub.) He loves to re -

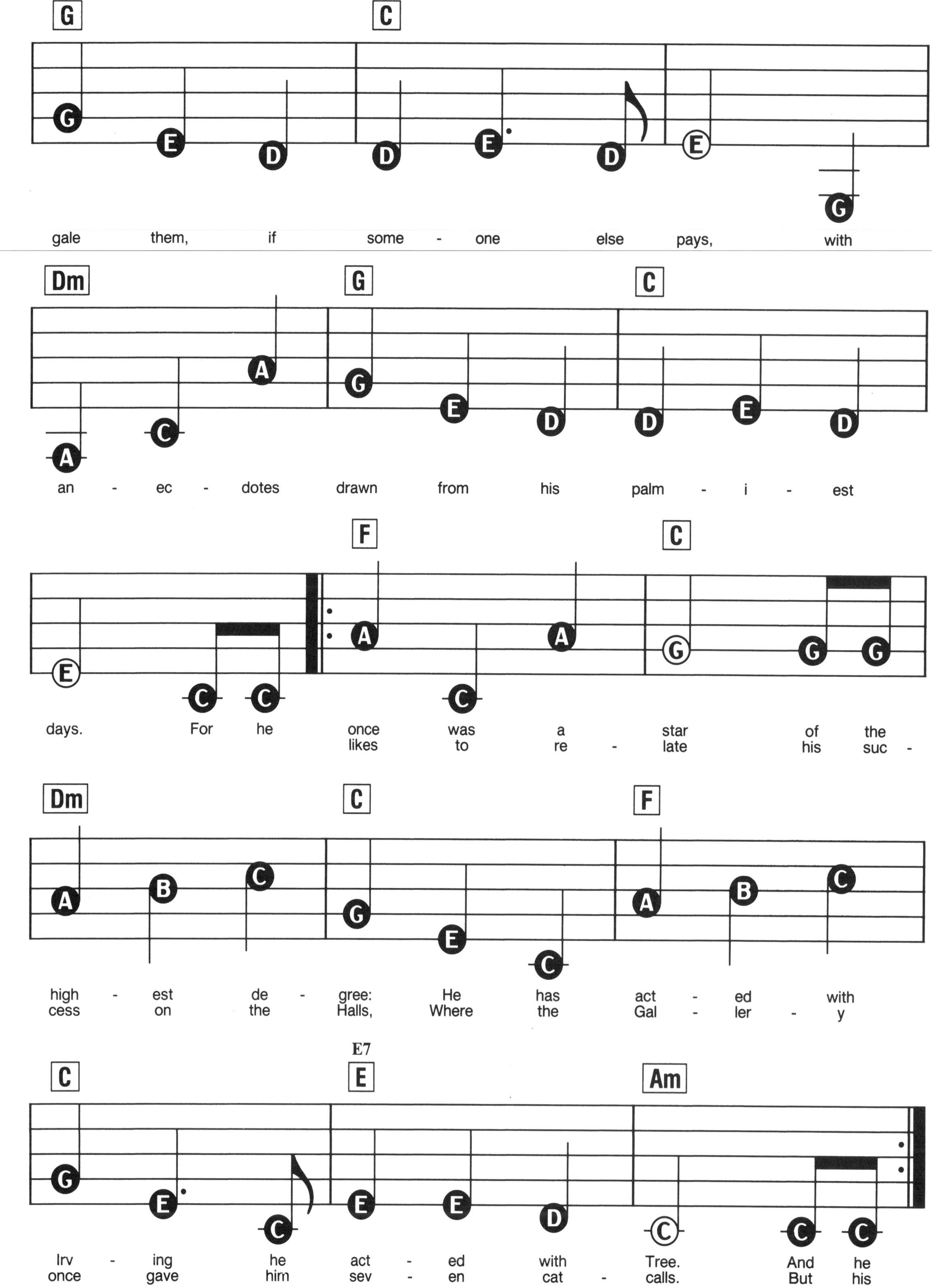
G C
gale them, if some - one else pays, with
Dm G C
an - ec - dotes drawn from his palm - i - est
F C
days. For he once was a star of the
likes to re - late his suc -
Dm C F
high - est de - gree: He has act - ed with
cess on the Halls, Where the Gal - ler - y
E7
C E Am
Irv - ing he act - ed with Tree. And he
once gave him sev - en cat - calls. But his

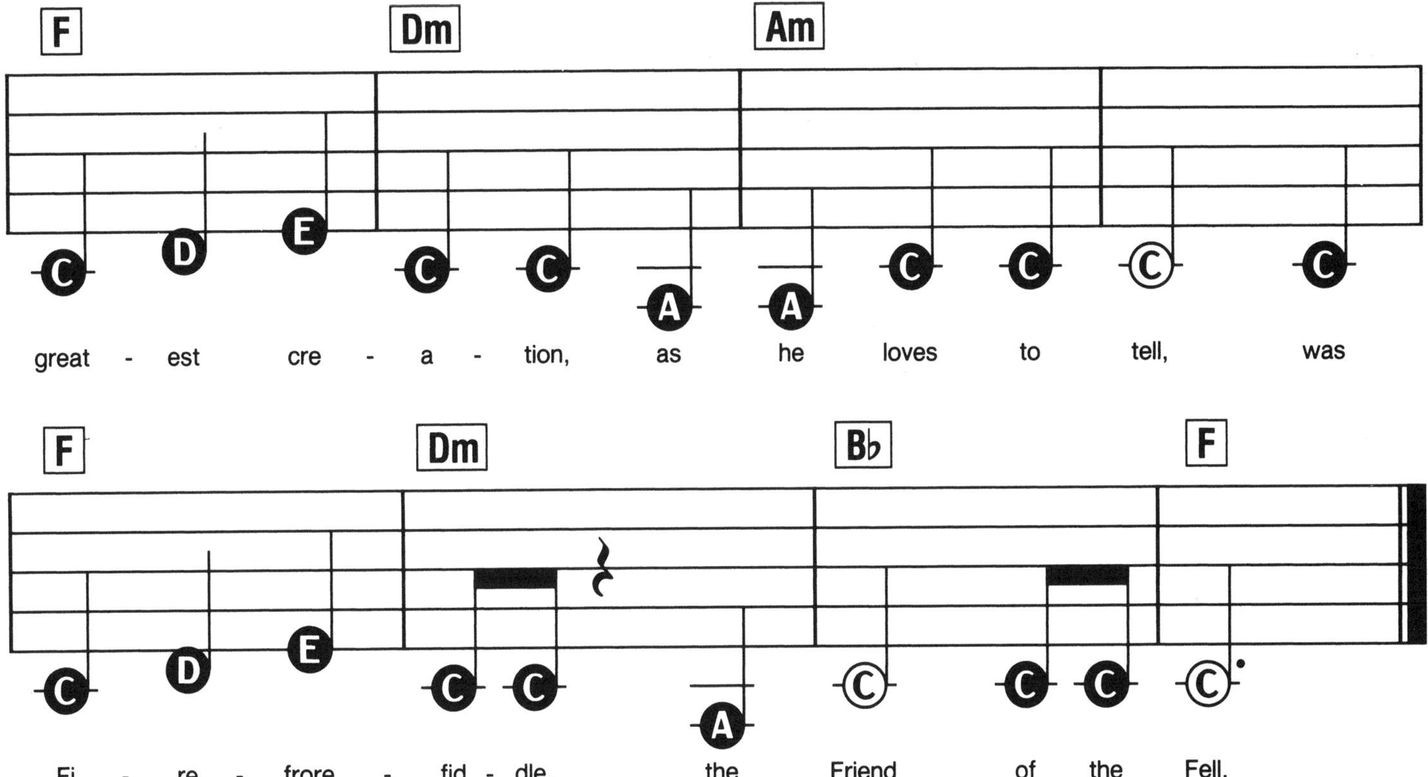

Additional Lyrics

"I have played in my time, ev'ry possible part,
And I used to know seventy speeches by heart.
I'd extemporize back-chat; I knew how to gag,
And I knew how to let the cat out of the bag.
I knew how to act with my back and my tail;
With an hour of rehearsal, I never could fail.
I'd a voice that would soften the hardest of hearts,
Whether I took the lead, or in character parts.
I have sat by the bedside of poor little Nell,
When the curfew was rung, then I swung on the bell.
In the pantomime season I never fell flat,
And I once understudied Dick Whittington's cat.
But my grandest creation, as hist'ry will tell,
Was Firefrorefiddle, the Fiend of the Fell."

Then, if someone will give him a toothful of gin,
He will tell how he once played a part in *East Lynne*.
At a Shakespeare performance he once walked on pat,
When some actor suggested the need for a cat.
And I say "Now these kittens, they do not get trained
As we did in the days when Victoria reigned.
They never get drilled in a regular troupe;
And they think they are smart just to jump through a hoop."
And he says as he scratches himself with his claws,
"Well the theatre is certainly not what it was.
These modern productions are all very well,
But there's nothing to equal, from what I hear tell,
That moment of mystery when I made history
As Firefrorefiddle, The Fiend of the Fell".

High Flying, Adored

from EVITA

Registration 4
Rhythm: Broadway or 8-Beat

Words by Tim Rice
Music by Andrew Lloyd Webber

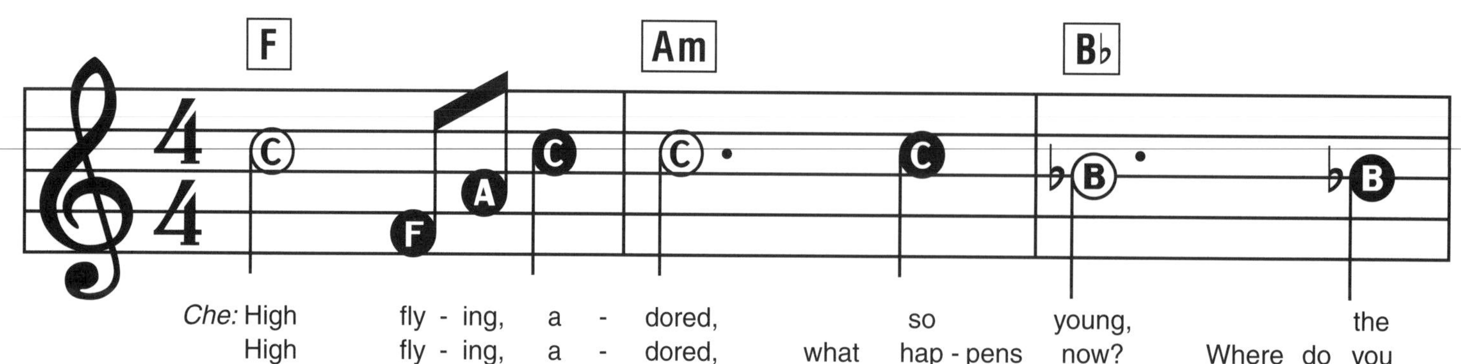

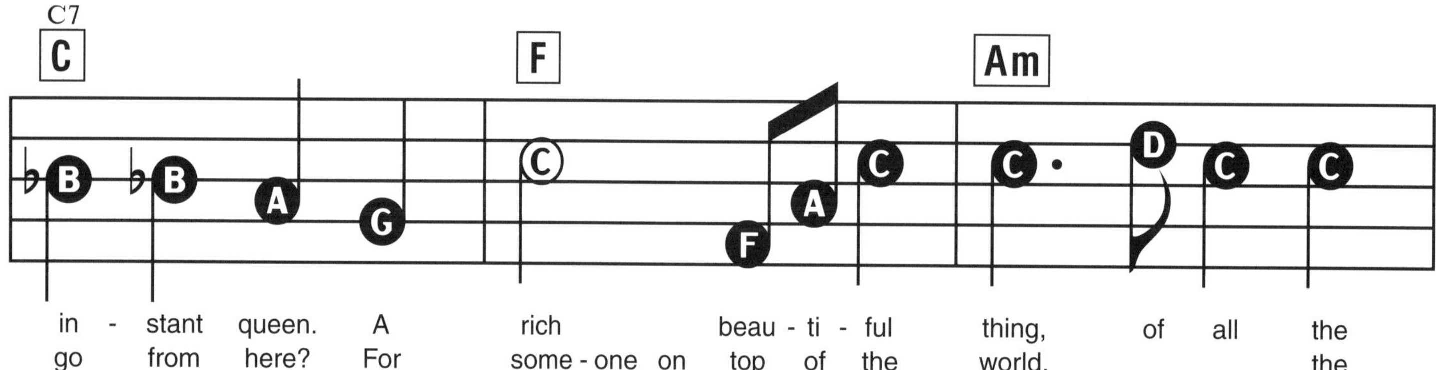

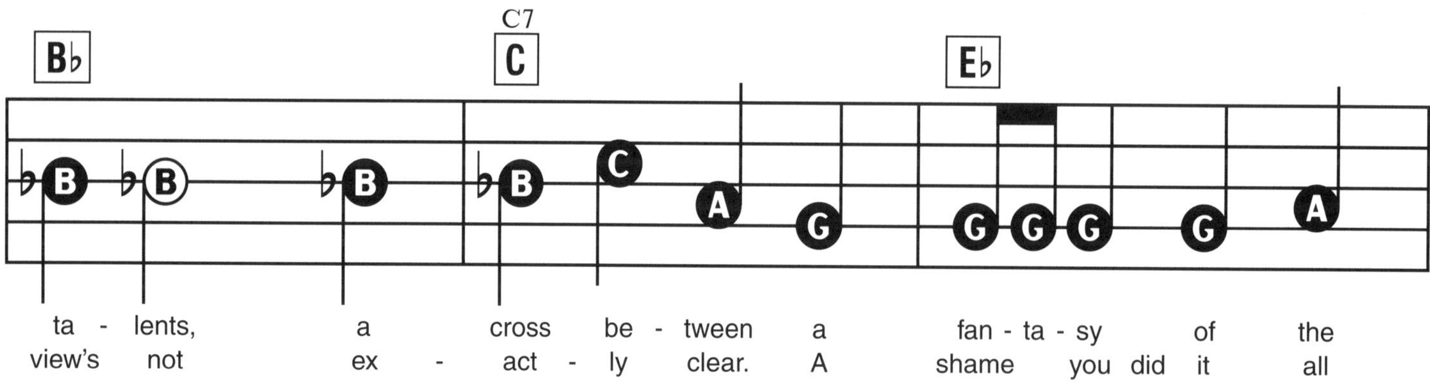

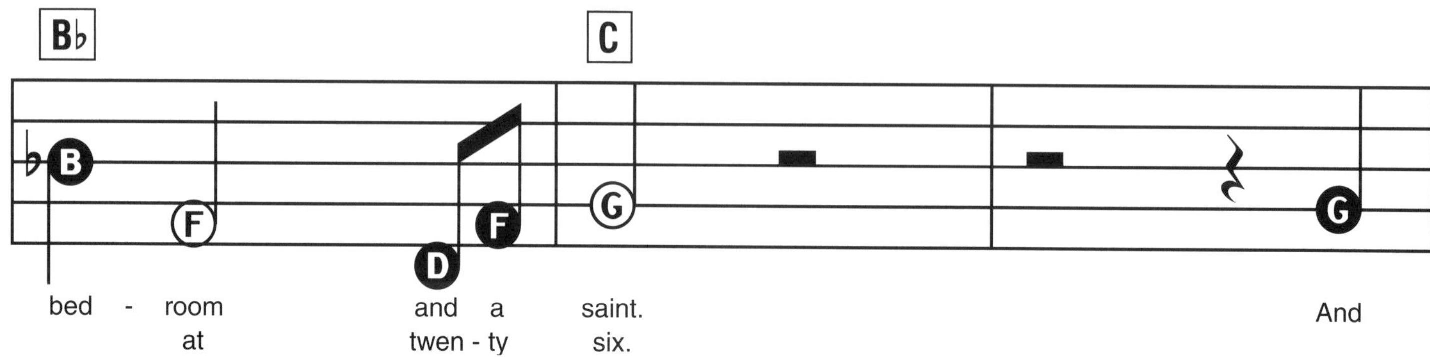

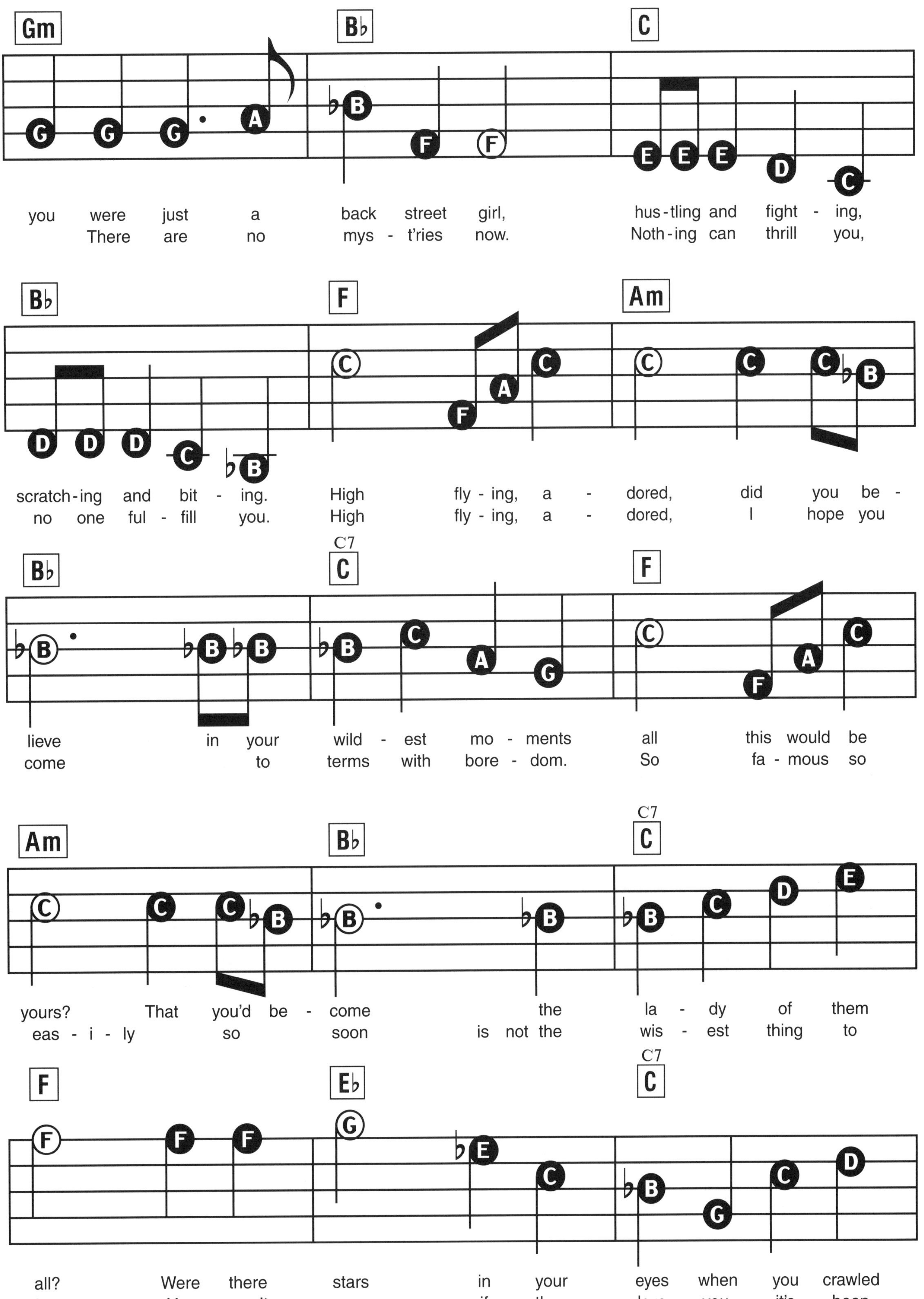
Gm
B♭
C
you were just a back street girl, hus-tling and fight - ing,
There are no mys - t'ries now. Noth-ing can thrill you,
B♭
F
Am
scratch-ing and bit - ing. High fly - ing, a - dored, did you be -
no one ful - fill you. High fly - ing, a - dored, I hope you
B♭
C7
C
F
lieve in your wild - est mo - ments all this would be
come to terms with bore - dom. So fa - mous so
Am
B♭
C7
C
yours? That you'd be - come the la - dy of them
eas - i - ly so soon is not the wis - est thing to
F
E♭
C7
C
all? Were there stars in your eyes when you crawled
be. You won't care if they love you, it's been

F
Eb
in at night
done be - fore.
from the bars, from the
You'll de - spair if they
C7
C
Am
Dm
Am
Dm
side - walks, from the gut - ter the - at - ri - cal?
hate you. You'll be drained of all en - er - gy.
Bb
F
Gm
Eb
Don't look down; it's a long, long way to fall.
All the young who've made it will a - gree.
Bb
F
Bb
F
(Instrumental)
C
Em
F
Eva:
High fly - ing, a - dored, I've been called names, but

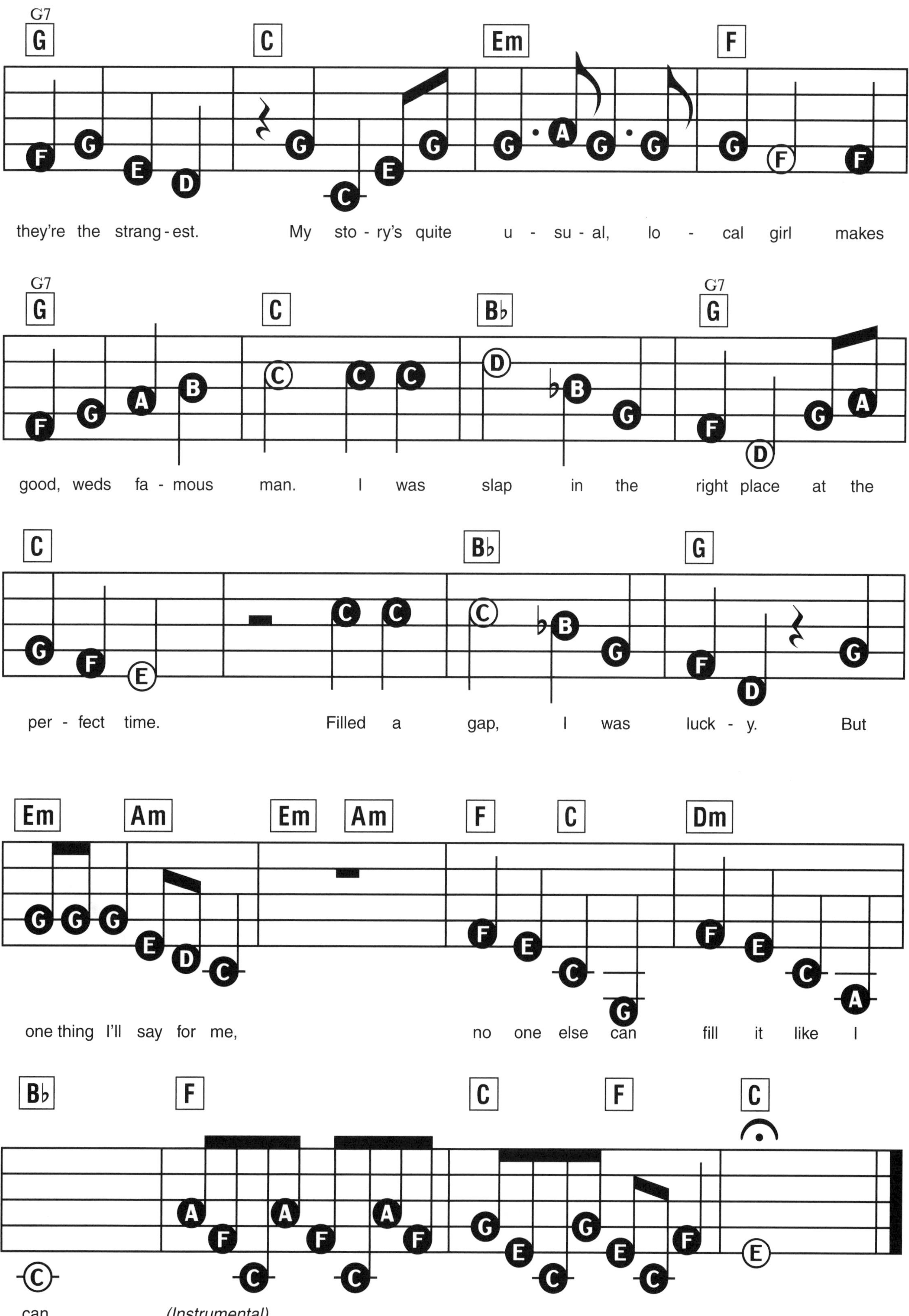
G7
G
C
Em
F
F G E D
G C E G
G A G G
G F F
they're the strang-est.
My sto-ry's quite
u-su-al,
lo-cal girl
makes
G7
G
C
B♭
G7
G
F G A B
C C C
D B G
F D G A
good, weds fa-mous
man.
I was
slap in the
right place at the
C
B♭
G
G F E
C C
C B G
F D G
per-fect time.
Filled a
gap, I was
luck-y.
But
Em
Am
Em
Am
F
C
Dm
G G G E D C
F E C G
F E C A
one thing I'll say for me,
no one else can
fill it like I
B♭
F
C
F
C
C
A F C A F C A F
G E C G E C F
E
can.
(Instrumental)

The Last Man in My Life

from SONG & DANCE

Registration 1
Rhythm: 4/4 Ballad

Music by Andrew Lloyd Webber
Lyrics by Don Black

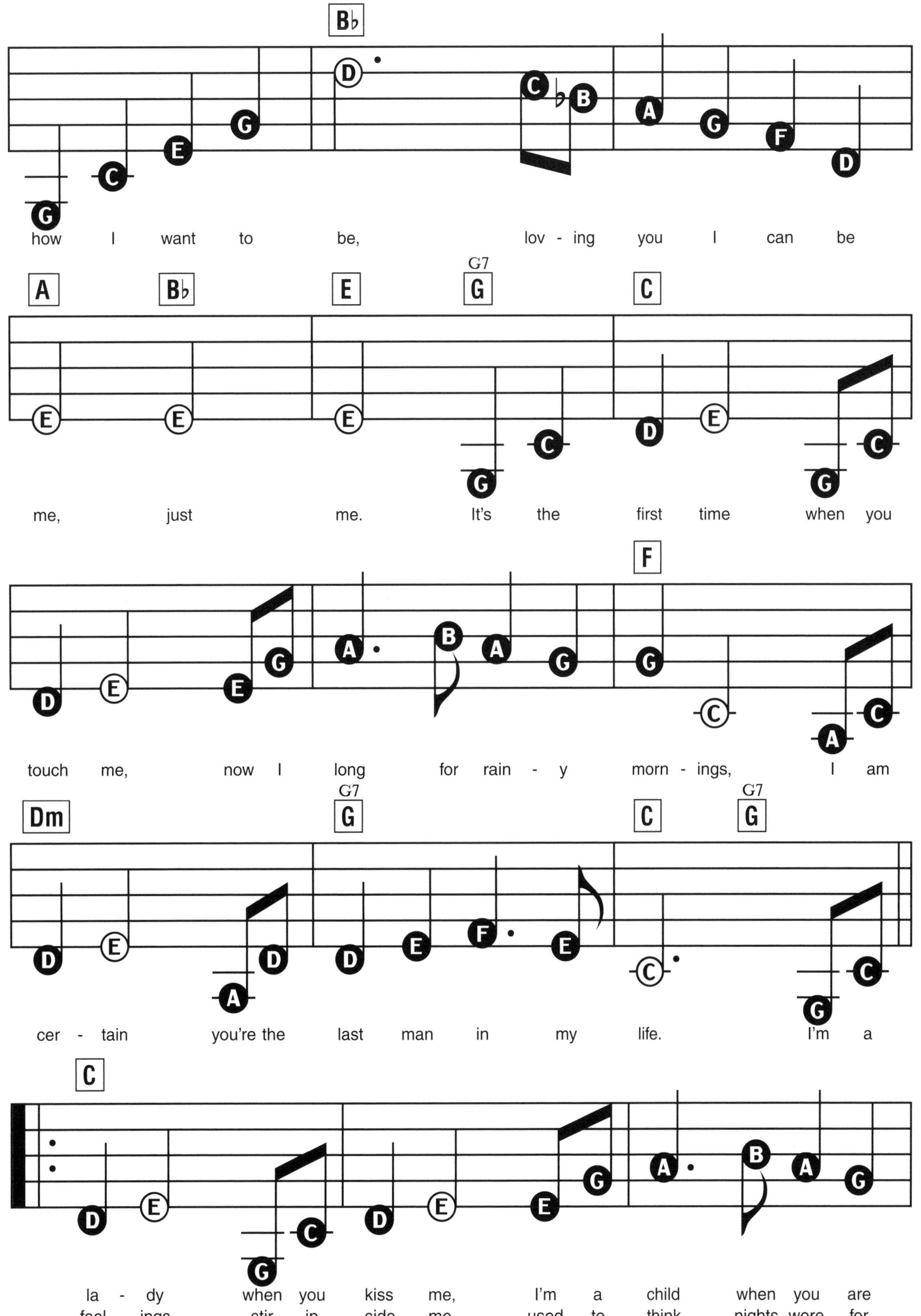
B♭
G C E G D C B A G F D
how I want to be, lov - ing you I can be
A B♭ E G7 G C
E E E G C D E G C
me, just me. It's the first time when you
F
D E E G A B A G G C A C
touch me, now I long for rain - y morn - ings, I am
Dm G7 G C G7 G
D E A D D E F E C G C
cer - tain you're the last man in my life. I'm a
C
D E G C D E E G A B A G
la - dy when you kiss me, I'm a child when you are
feel - ings stir in - side me, used to think nights were for

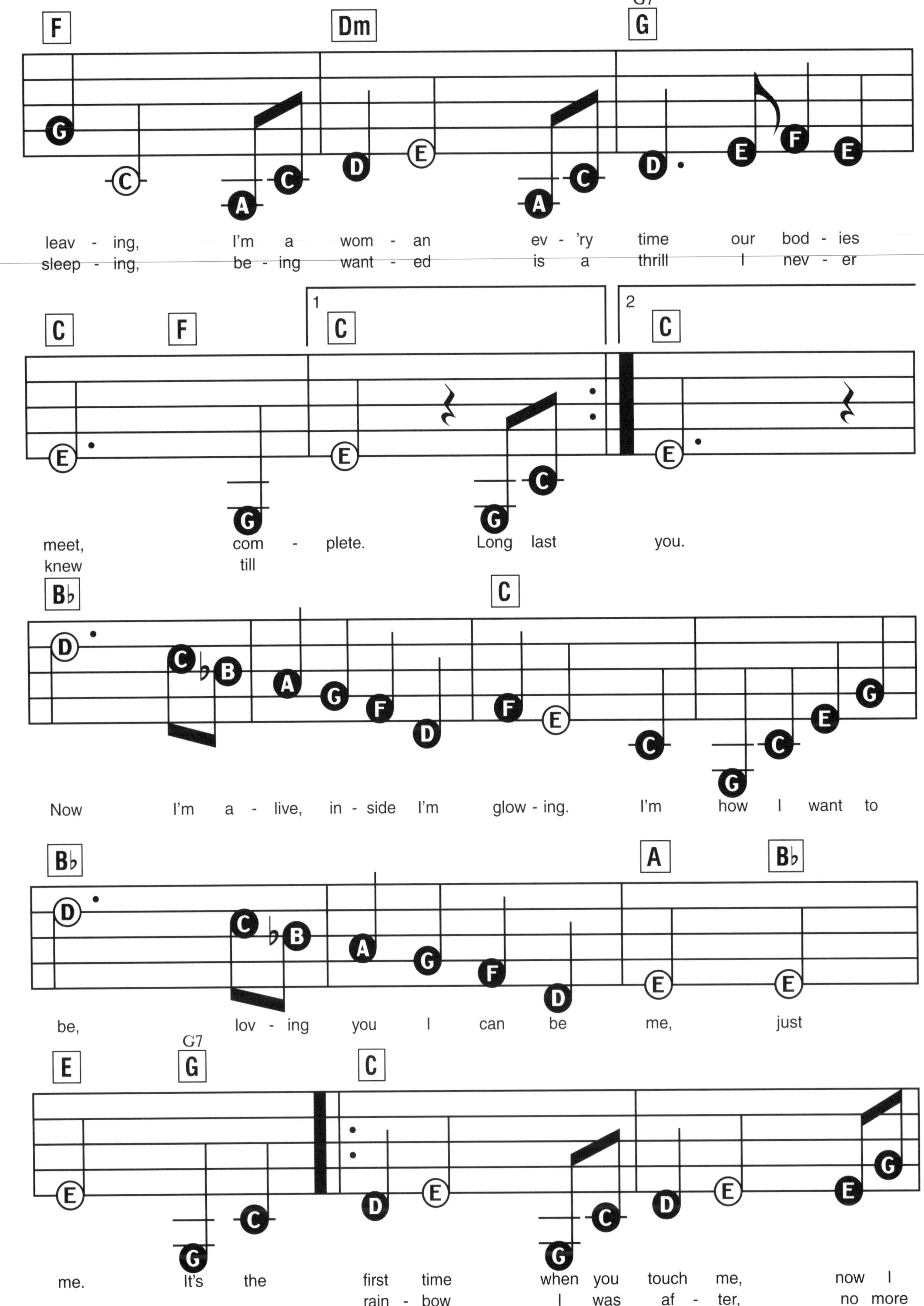
F Dm G7 G
leav - ing, I'm a wom - an ev - 'ry time our bod - ies
sleep - ing, be - ing want - ed is a thrill I nev - er
C F 1 C 2 C
meet, com - plete. Long last you.
knew till
B♭ C
Now I'm a - live, in - side I'm glow - ing. I'm how I want to
B♭ A B♭
be, lov - ing you I can be me, just
E G7 G C
me. It's the first time when you touch me, now I
rain - bow I was af - ter, no more

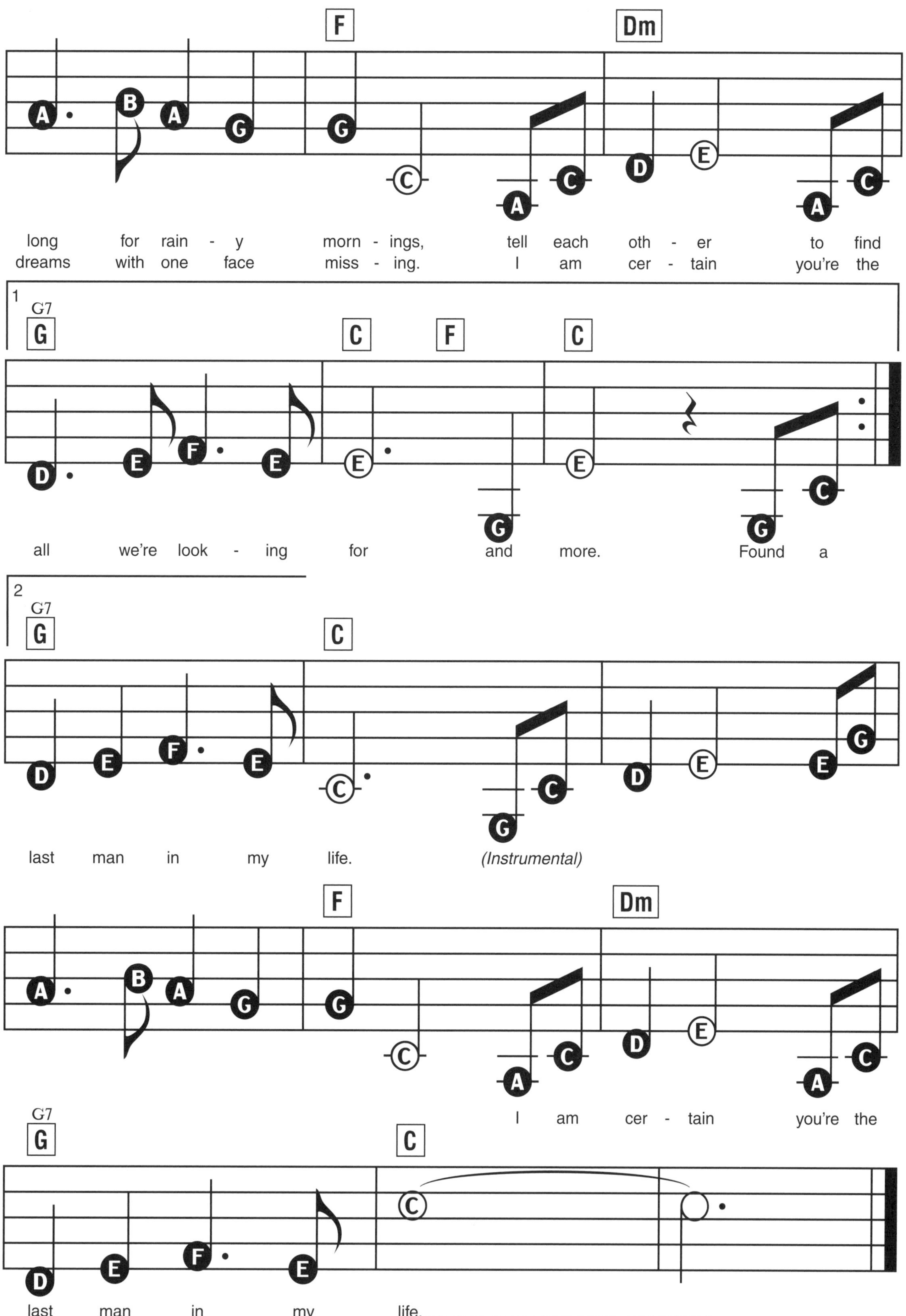
F
Dm
long for rain - y morn - ings, tell each oth - er to find
dreams with one face miss - ing. I am cer - tain you're the
1
G7
G
C
F
C
all we're look - ing for and more. Found a
2
G7
G
C
last man in my life. (Instrumental)
F
Dm
I am cer - tain you're the
G7
G
C
last man in my life.

The Perfect Year

from SUNSET BOULEVARD

Registration 3
Rhythm: None

Music by Andrew Lloyd Webber
Lyrics by Don Black and Christopher Hampton

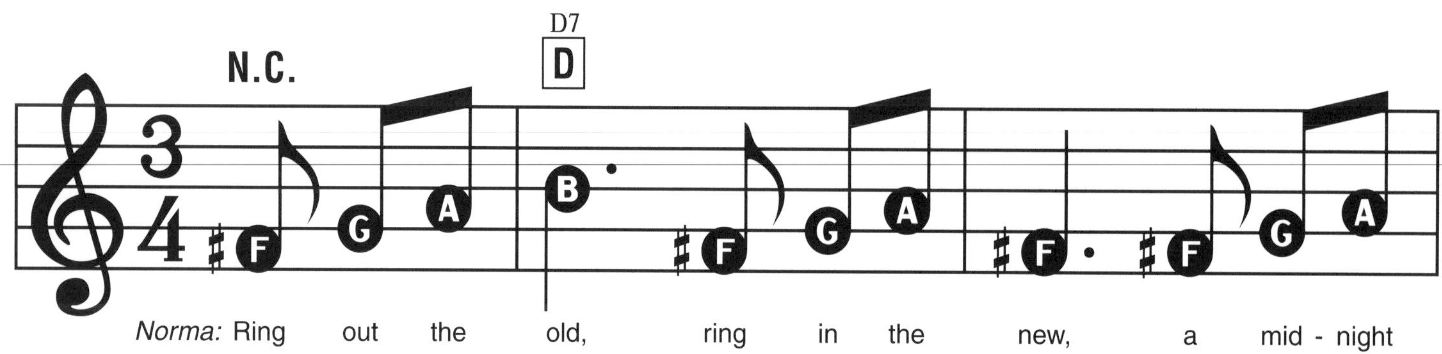
N.C.
D7
D
3
4
F G A B F G A F F G A
Norma: Ring out the old, ring in the new, a mid - night

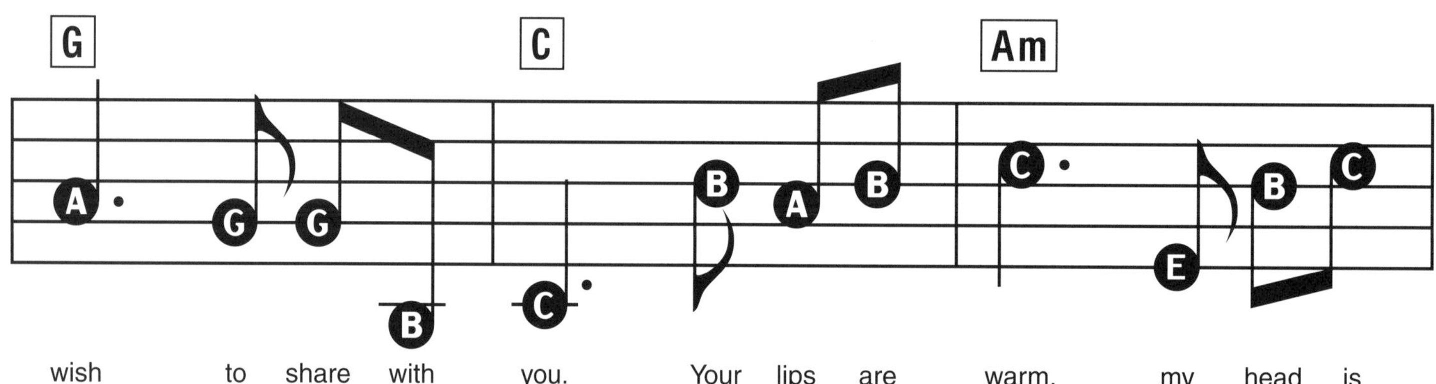
G
C
Am
A G G B C B A B C E B C
wish to share with you. Your lips are warm, my head is

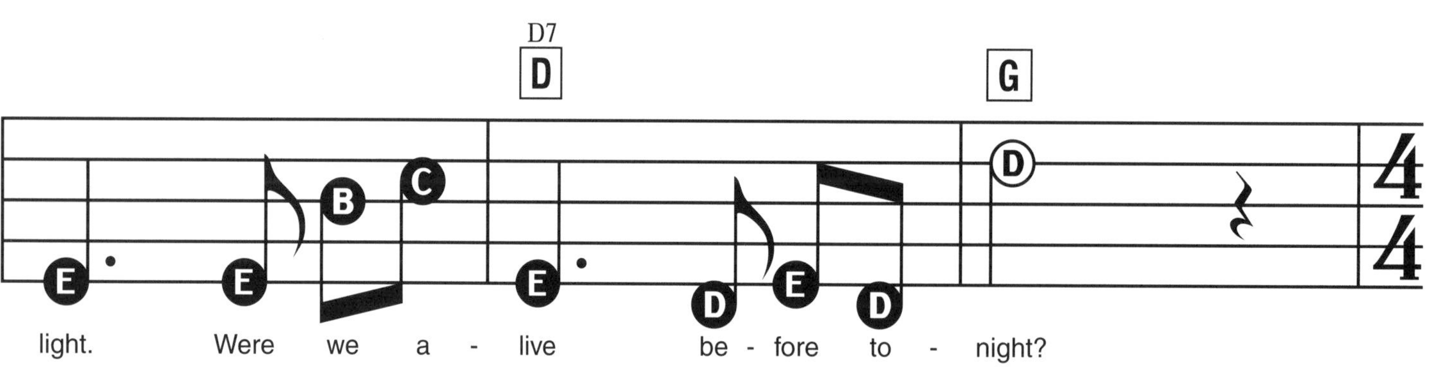
D7
D
G
E E B C E D E D D
light. Were we a - live be - fore to - night?

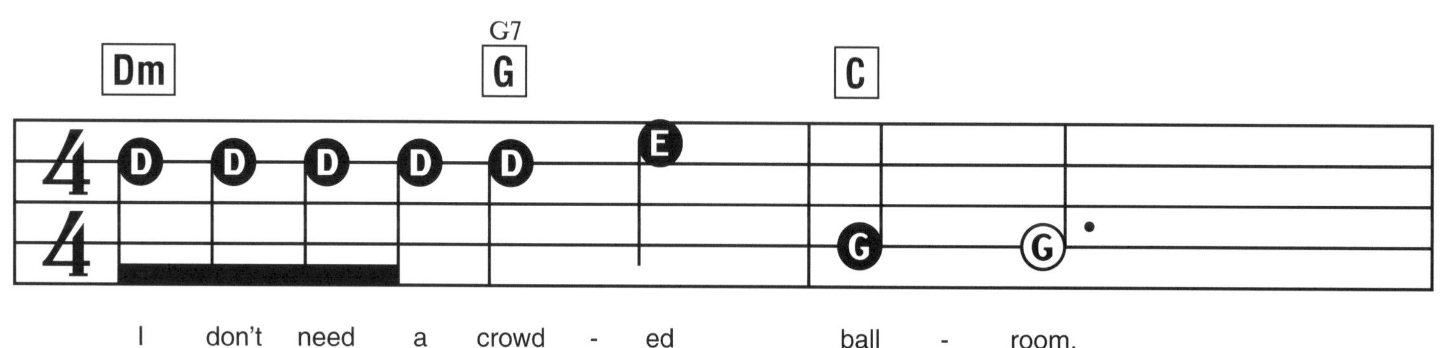
Dm
G7
G
C
4
4
D D D D D E G G
I don't need a crowd - ed ball - room,

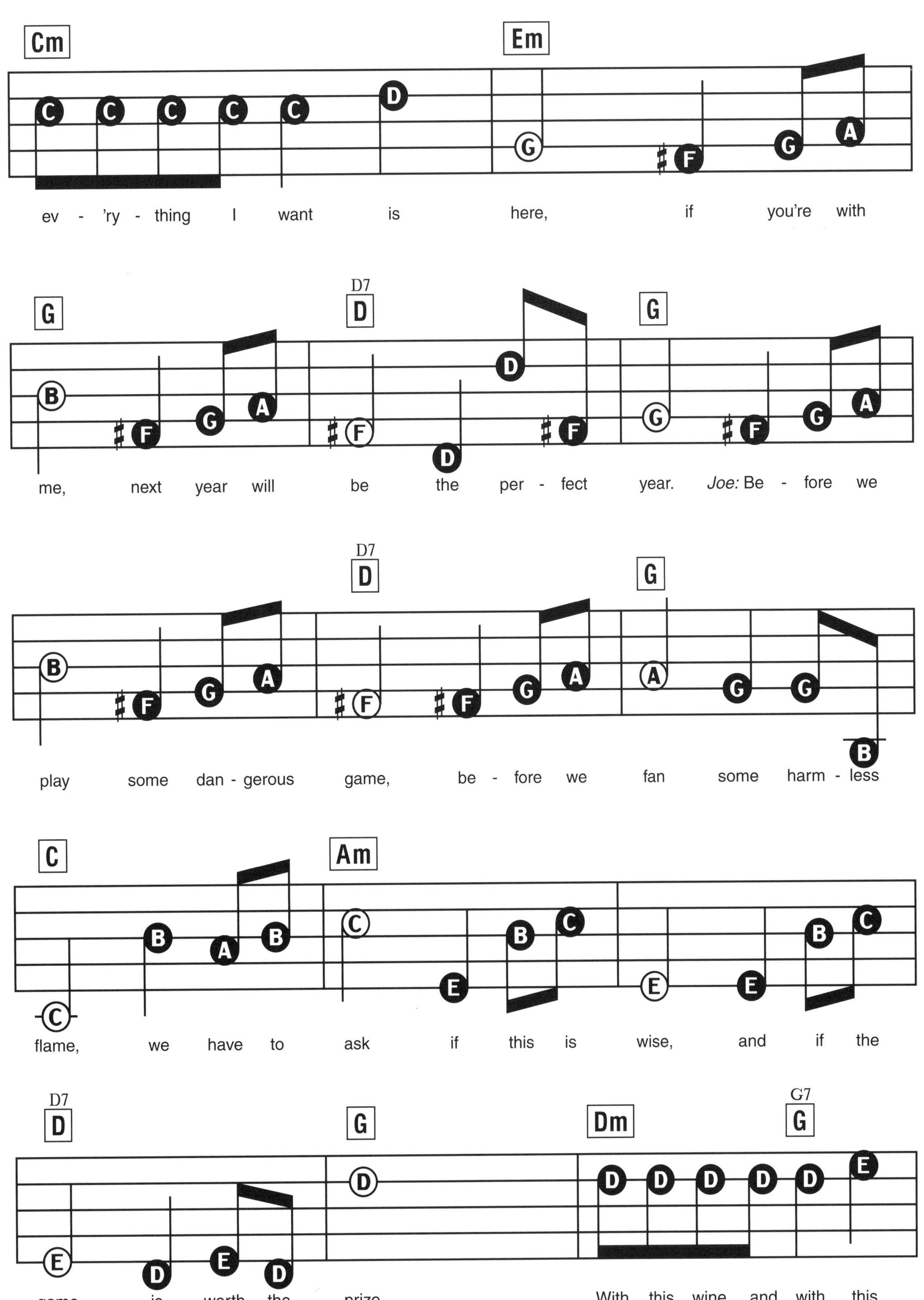
Cm
Em
ev - 'ry - thing I want is here, if you're with
G
D7
D
G
me, next year will be the per - fect year. Joe: Be - fore we
D7
D
G
play some dan - gerous game, be - fore we fan some harm - less
C
Am
flame, we have to ask if this is wise, and if the
D7
D
G
Dm
G7
G
game is worth the prize. With this wine, and with this

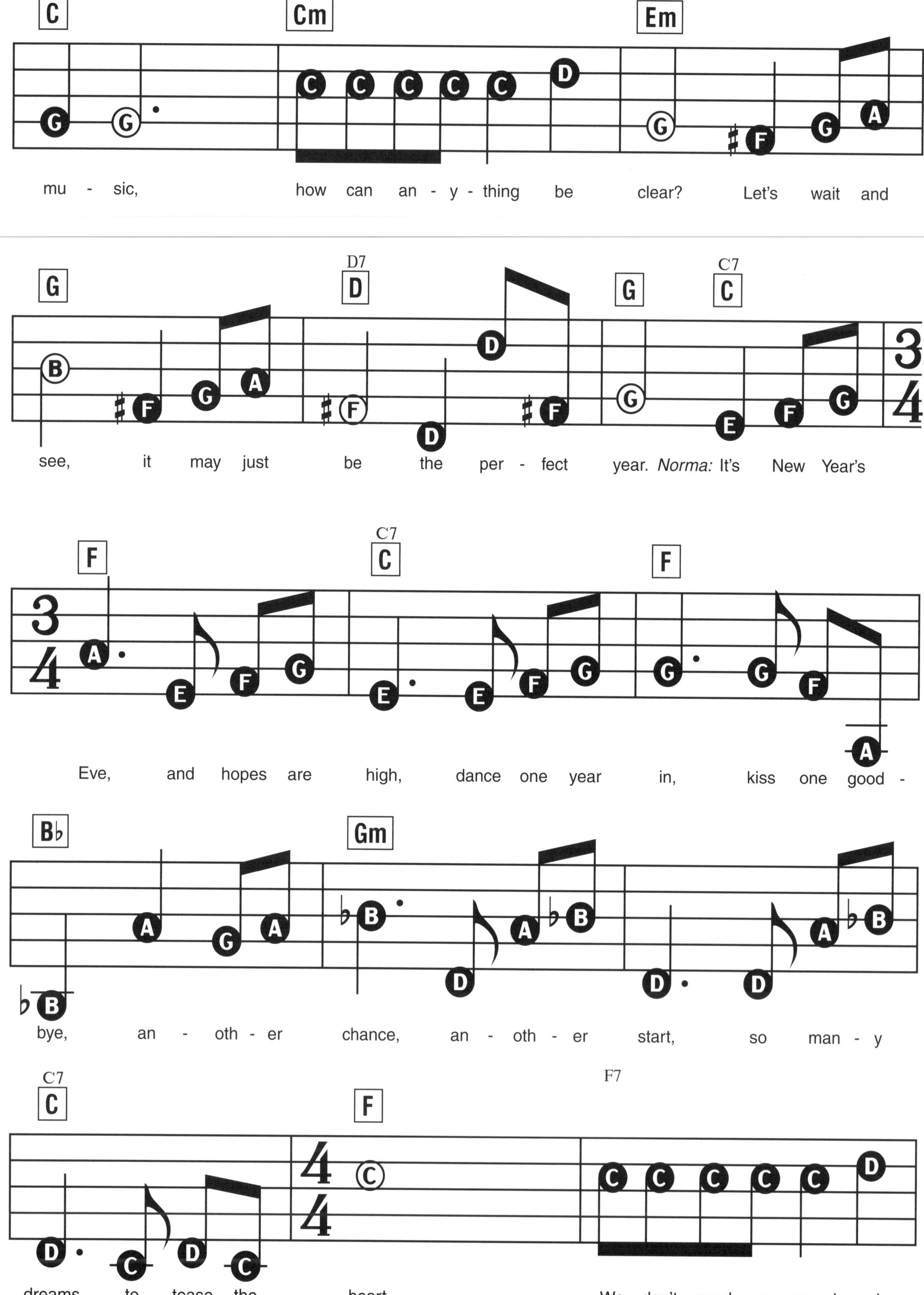
C
Cm
Em
mu - sic,
how can an - y - thing be
clear? Let's wait and
G
D7
D
G
C7
C
see, it may just
be the per - fect
year. Norma: It's New Year's
F
C7
C
F
Eve, and hopes are
high, dance one year
in, kiss one good -
B♭
Gm
bye, an - oth - er
chance, an - oth - er
start, so man - y
C7
C
F
F7
dreams to tease the
heart.
We don't need a crowd - ed

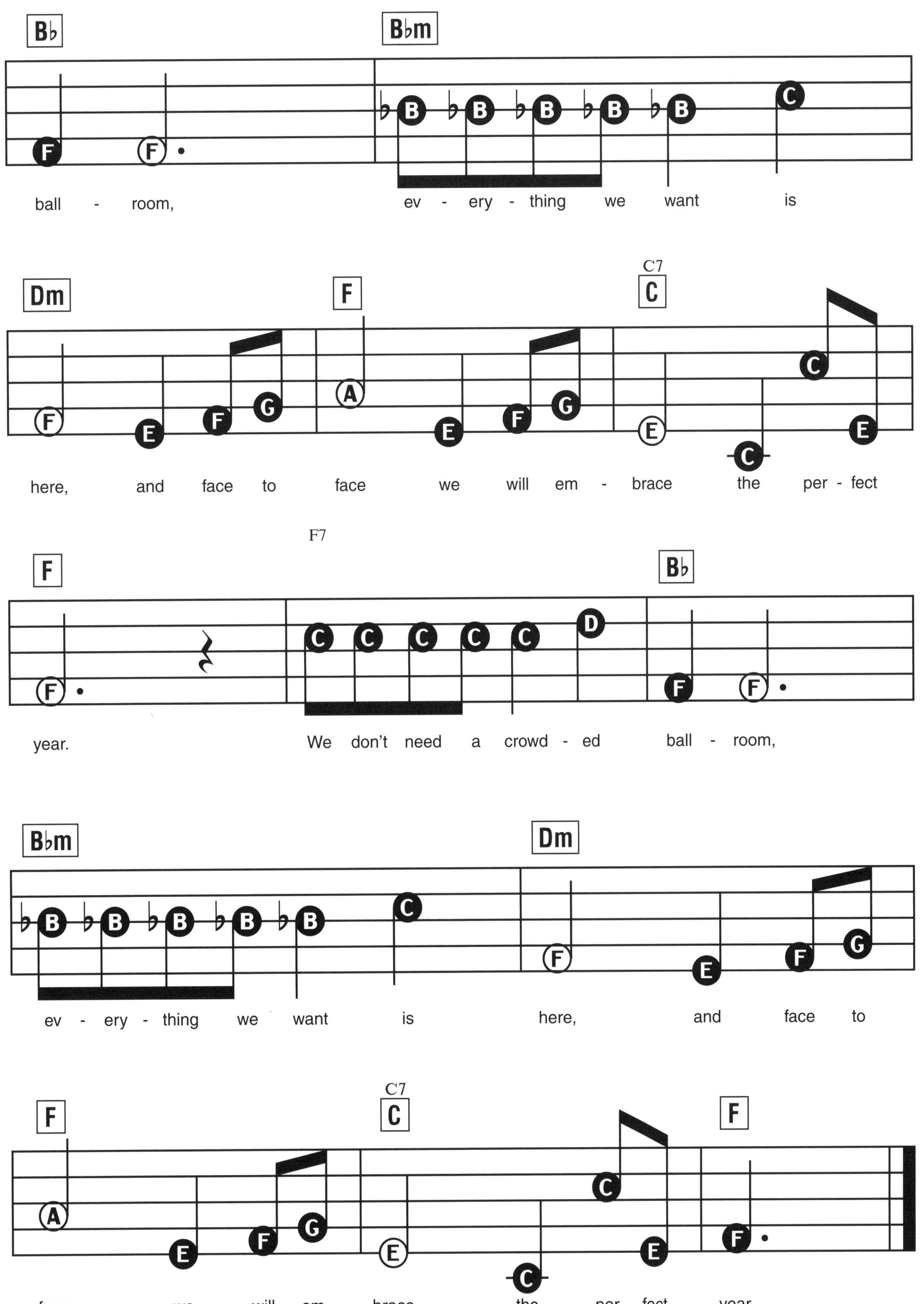
B♭
B♭m
ball - room,
ev - ery - thing we want is
Dm
F
C7
C
here, and face to face we will em - brace the per - fect
F
F7
B♭
year. We don't need a crowd - ed ball - room,
B♭m
Dm
ev - ery - thing we want is here, and face to
F
C7
C
F
face we will em - brace the per - fect year.

Pie Jesu
from REQUIEM

Registration 3
Rhythm: No Rhythm

By Andrew Lloyd Webber

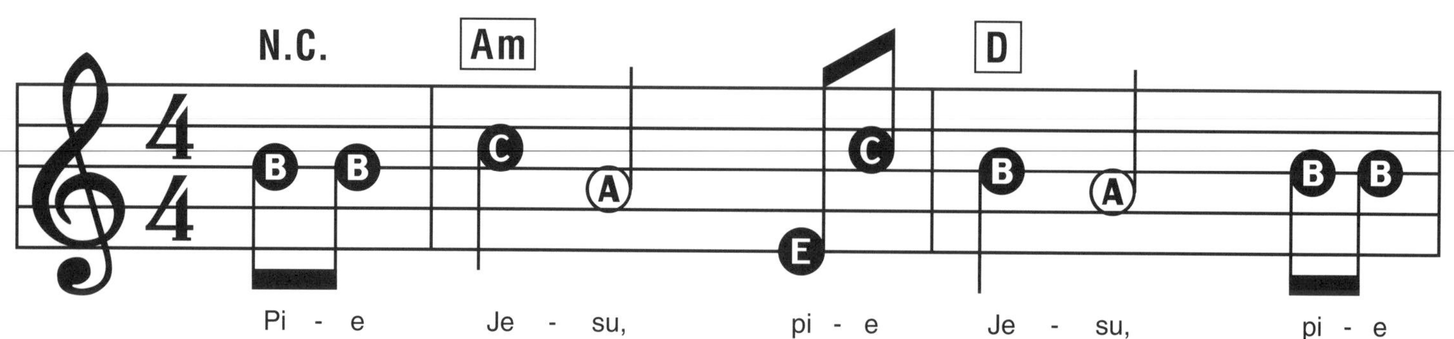

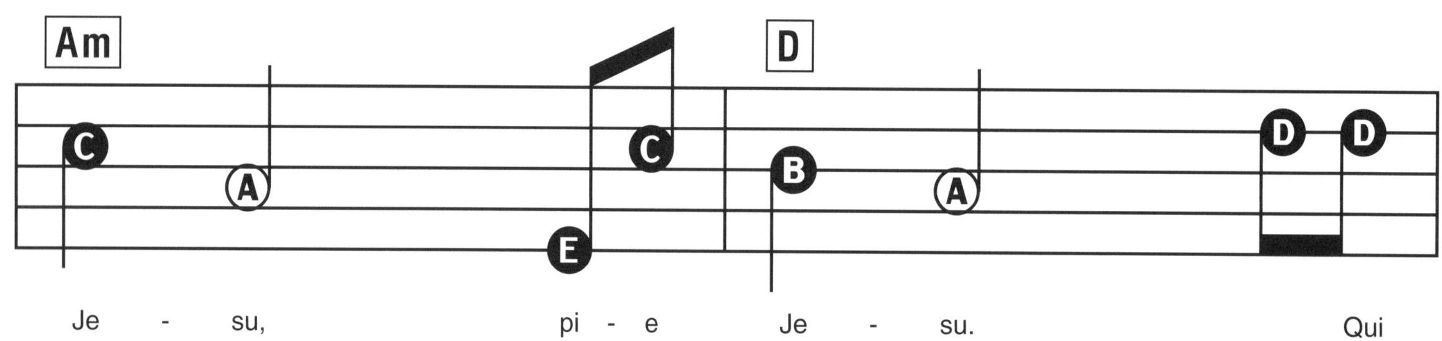

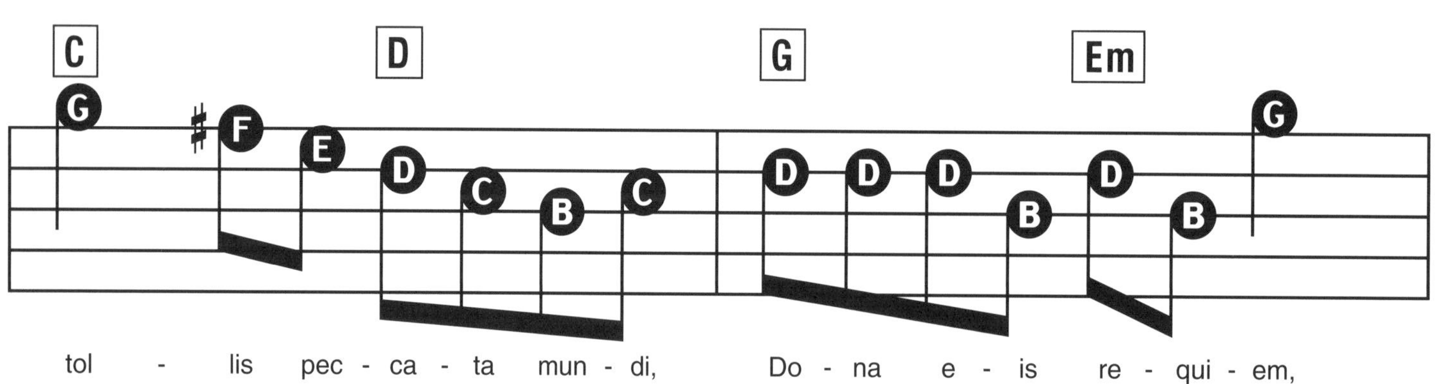

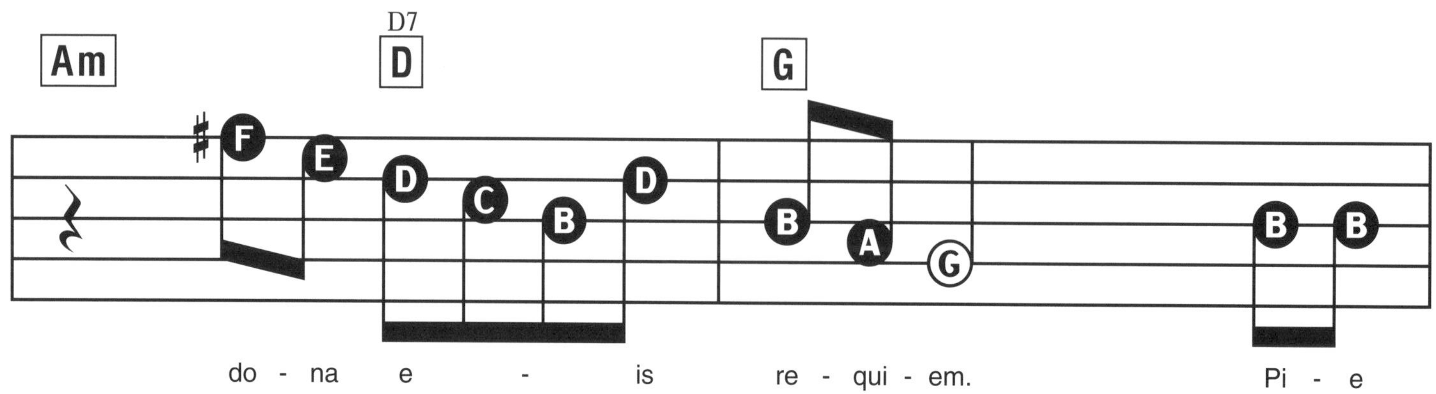

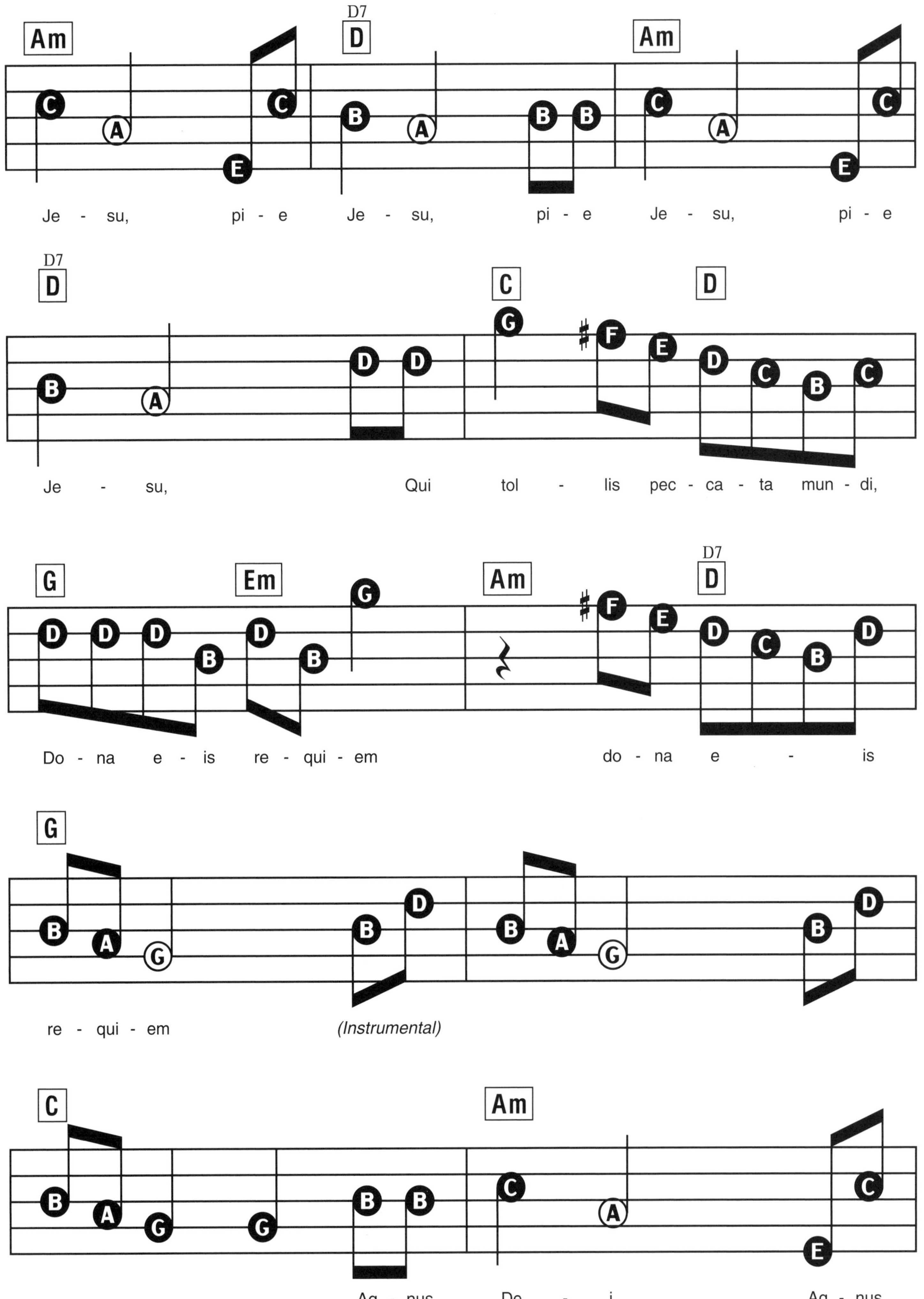
Am
D7
D
Am
Je - su, pi - e Je - su, pi - e Je - su, pi - e
D7
D
C
D
Je - su, Qui tol - lis pec - ca - ta mun - di,
G
Em
Am
D7
D
Do - na e - is re - qui - em do - na e - is
G
re - qui - em (Instrumental)
C
Am
Ag - nus De - i, Ag - nus

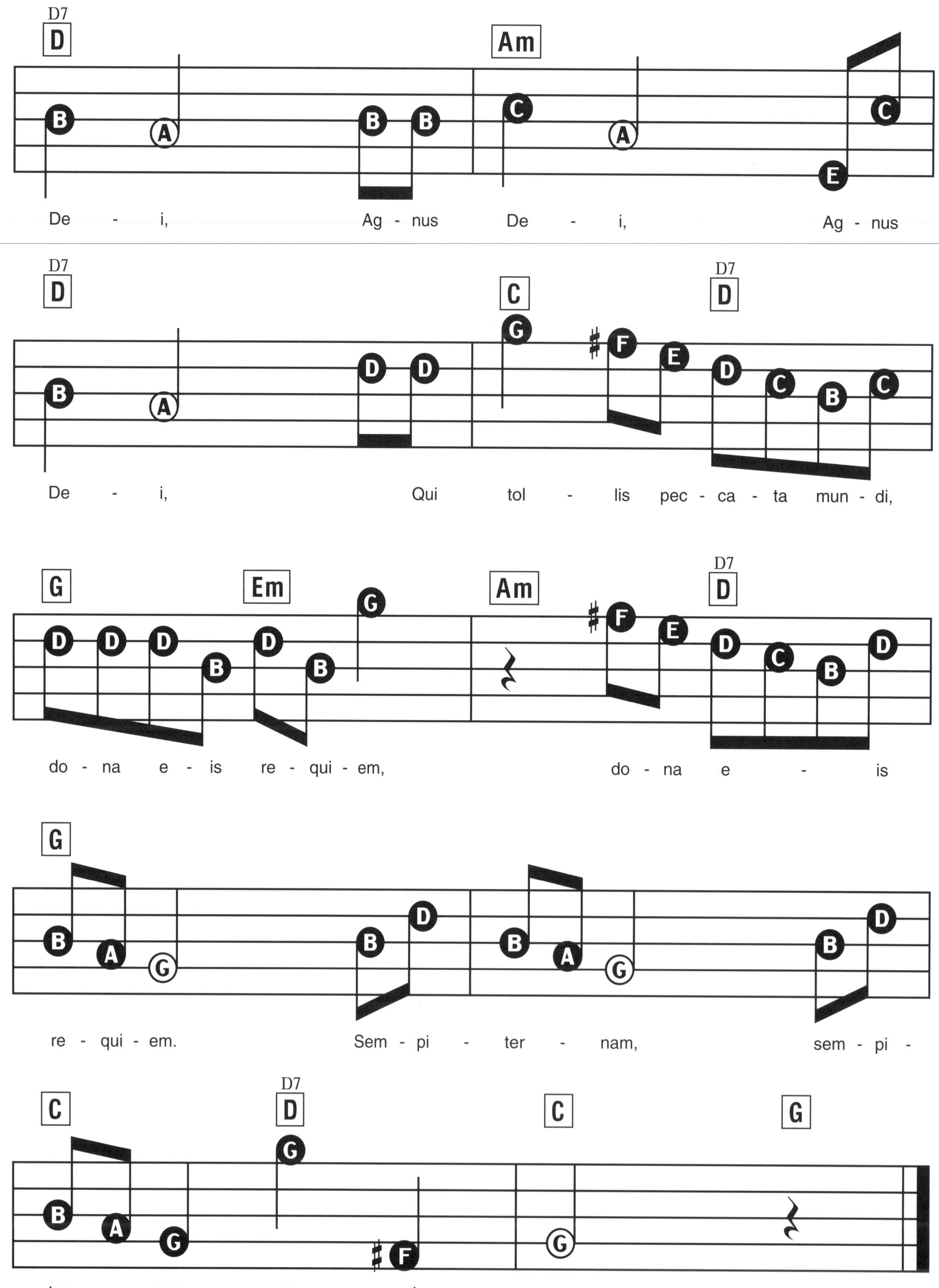
D7 D Am
De - i, Ag - nus De - i, Ag - nus
D7 D C D7 D
De - i, Qui tol - lis pec - ca - ta mun - di,
G Em Am D7 D
do - na e - is re - qui - em, do - na e - is
G
re - qui - em. Sem - pi - ter - nam, sem - pi -
C D7 D C G
ter - nam, re - qui - em.

The Point of No Return

from THE PHANTOM OF THE OPERA

Registration 1
Rhythm: Waltz

Music by Andrew Lloyd Webber
Lyrics by Charles Hart
Additional Lyrics by Richard Stilgoe

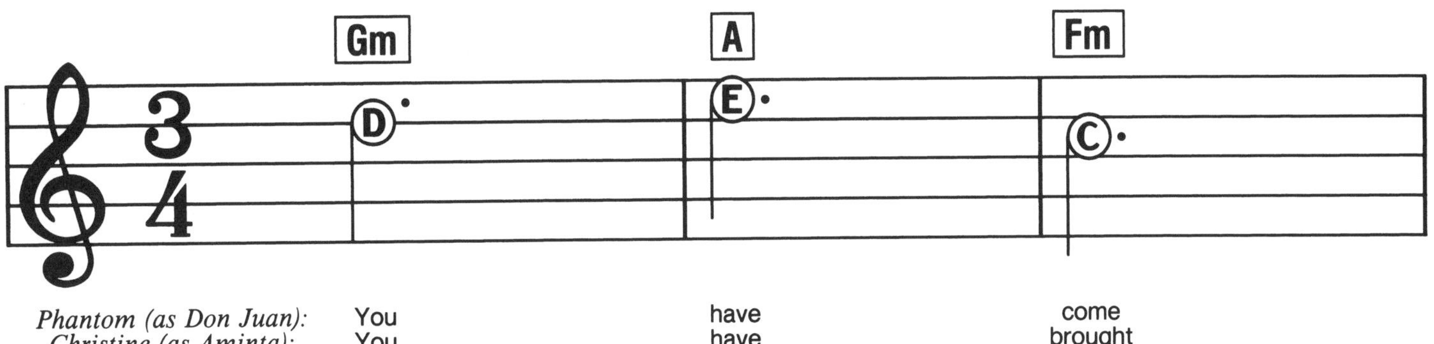

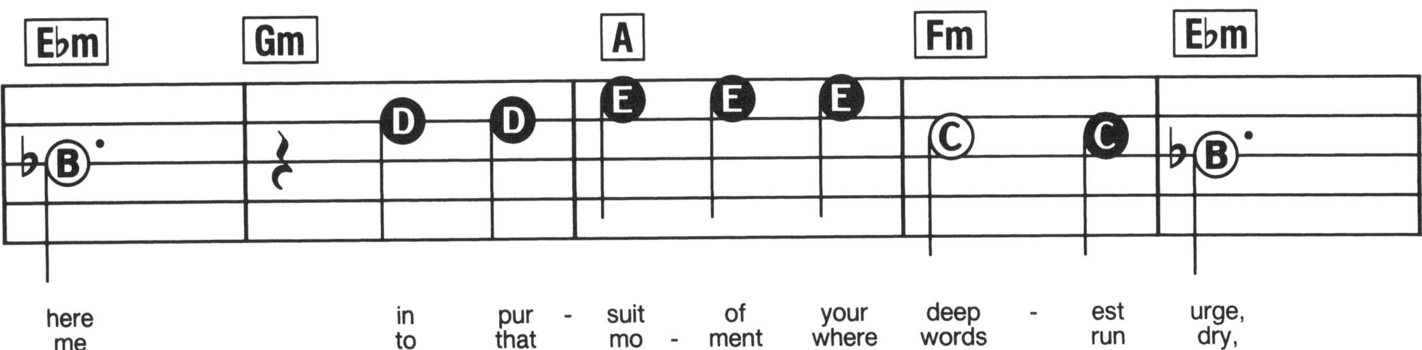

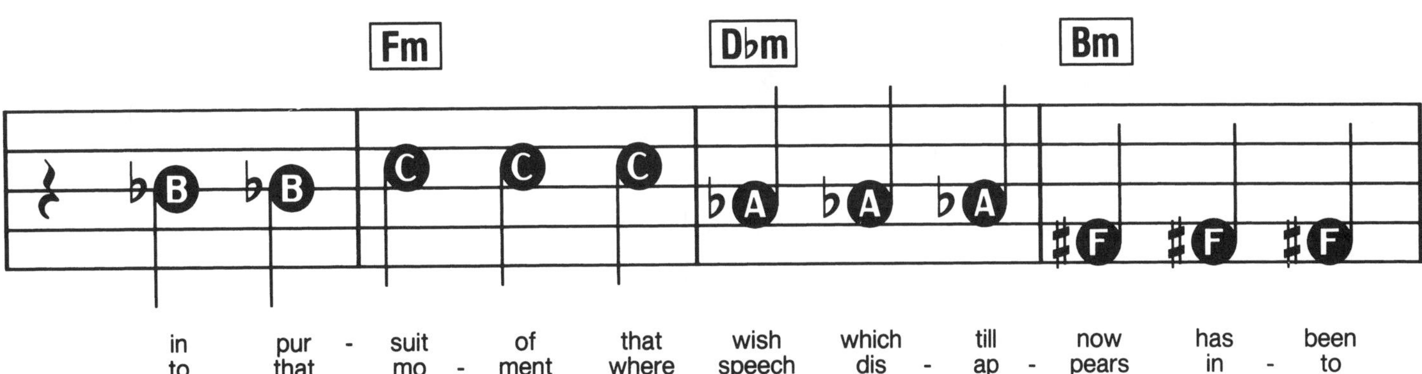

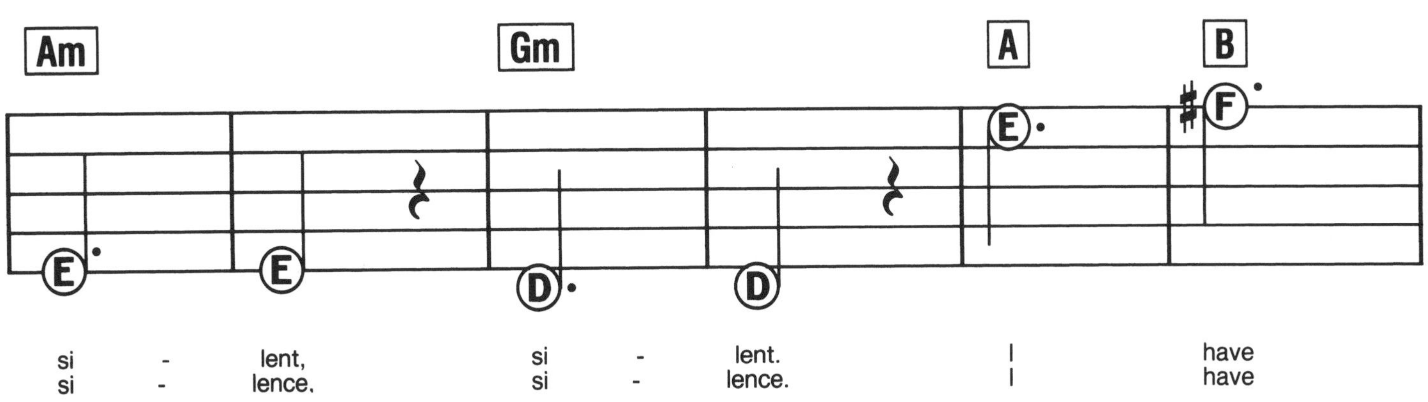

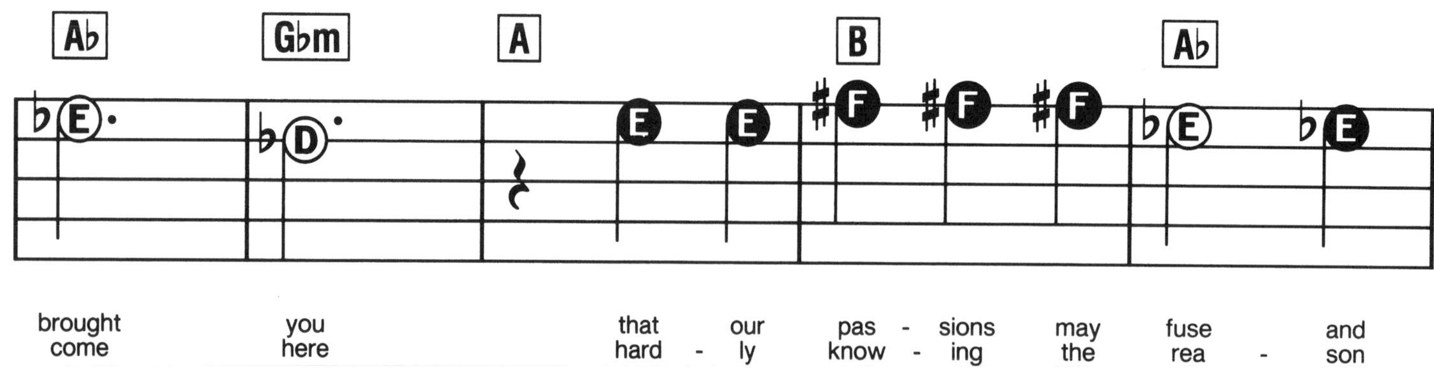
Ab Gbm A B Ab
brought you that our pas - sions may fuse and
come here hard - ly know - ing the rea - son

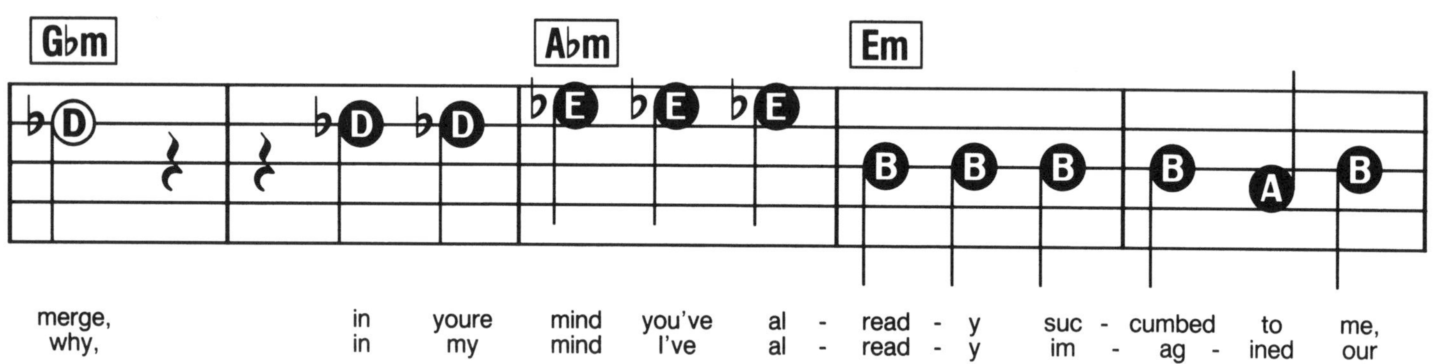
Gbm Abm Em
merge, in youre mind you've al - read - y suc - cumbed to me,
why, in my mind I've al - read - y im - ag - ined our

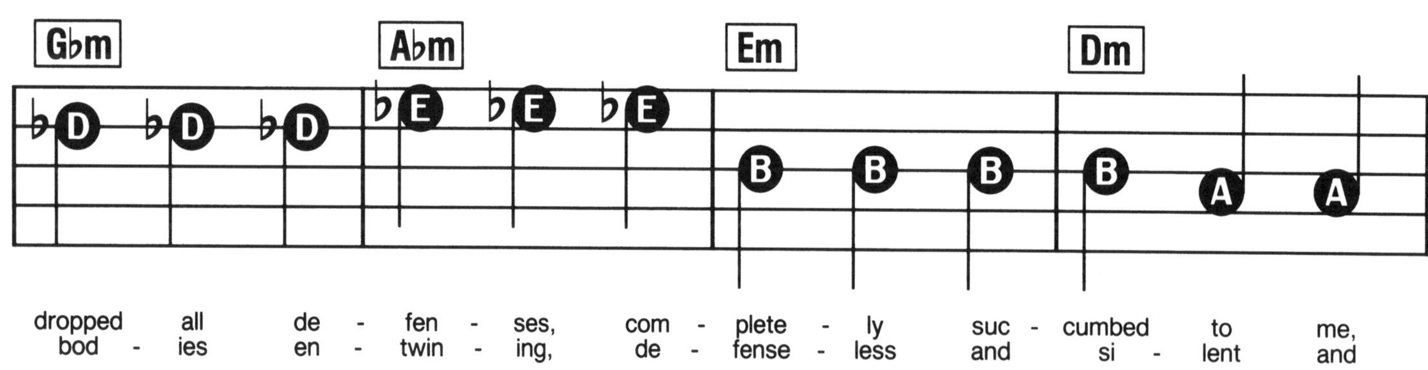
Gbm Abm Em Dm
dropped all de - fen - ses, com - plete - ly suc - cumbed to me,
bod - ies en - twin - ing, de - fense - less and si - lent and

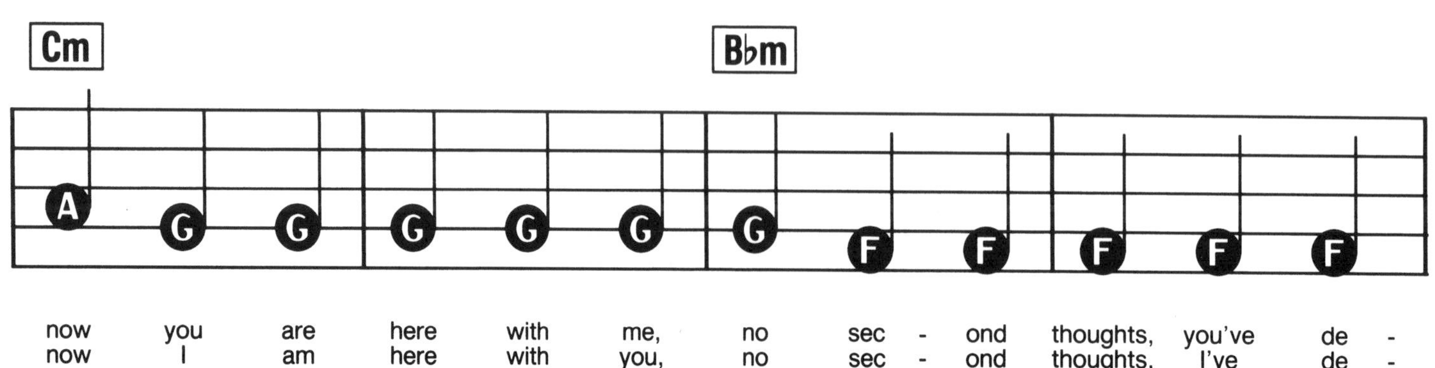
Cm Bbm
now you are here with me, no sec - ond thoughts, you've de -
now I am here with you, no sec - ond thoughts, I've de -

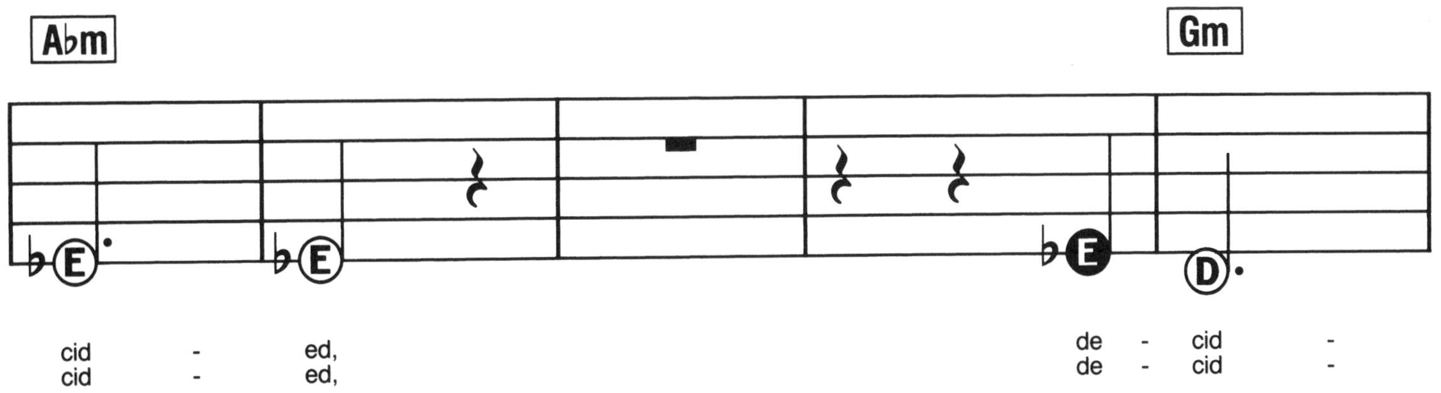
A♭m
Gm
cid - ed, de - cid -
cid - ed, de - cid -

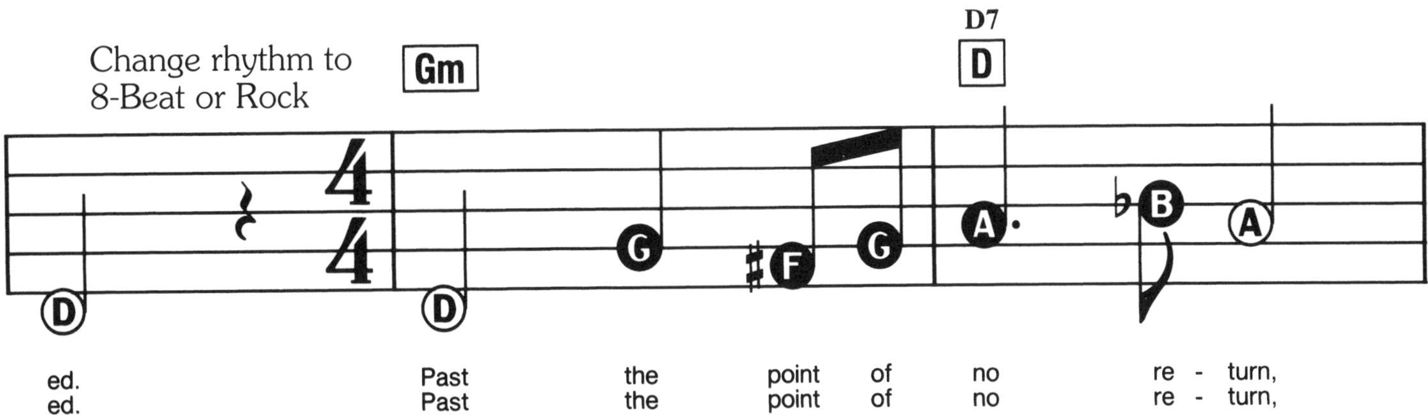
Change rhythm to
8-Beat or Rock
Gm
D7
D
ed. Past the point of no re - turn,
ed. Past the point of no re - turn,

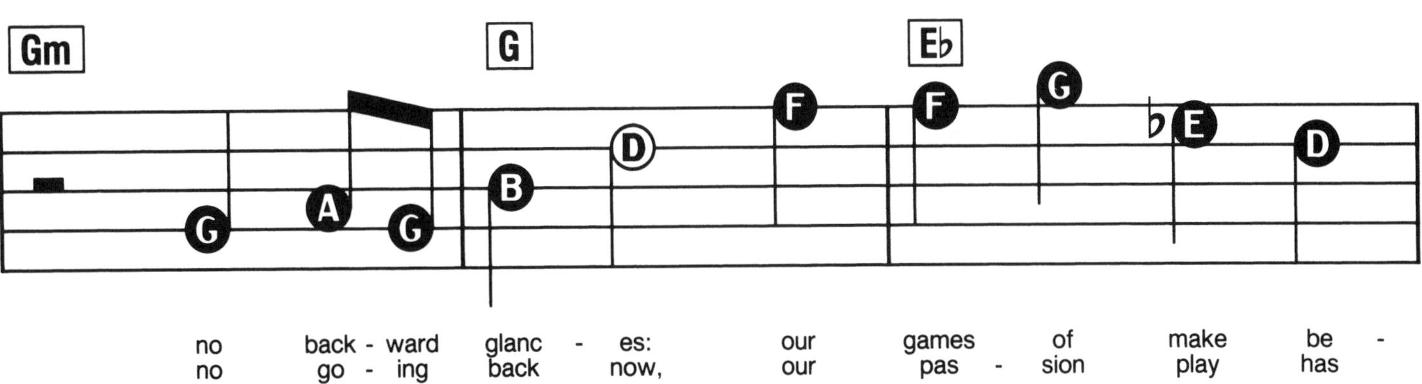
Gm
G
E♭
no back - ward glanc - es: our games of make be -
no go - ing back now, our pas - sion play has

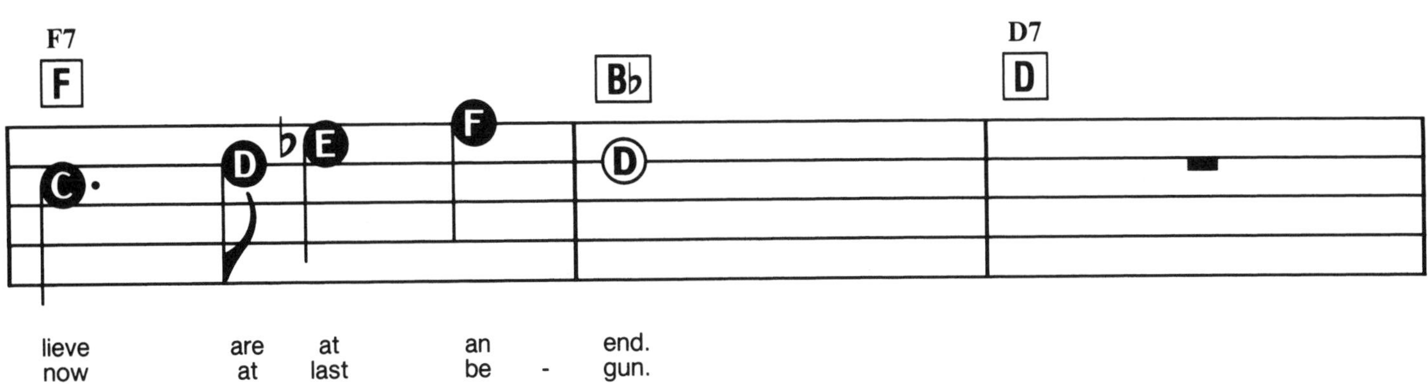
F7
F
B♭
D7
D
lieve are at an end.
now at last be - gun.

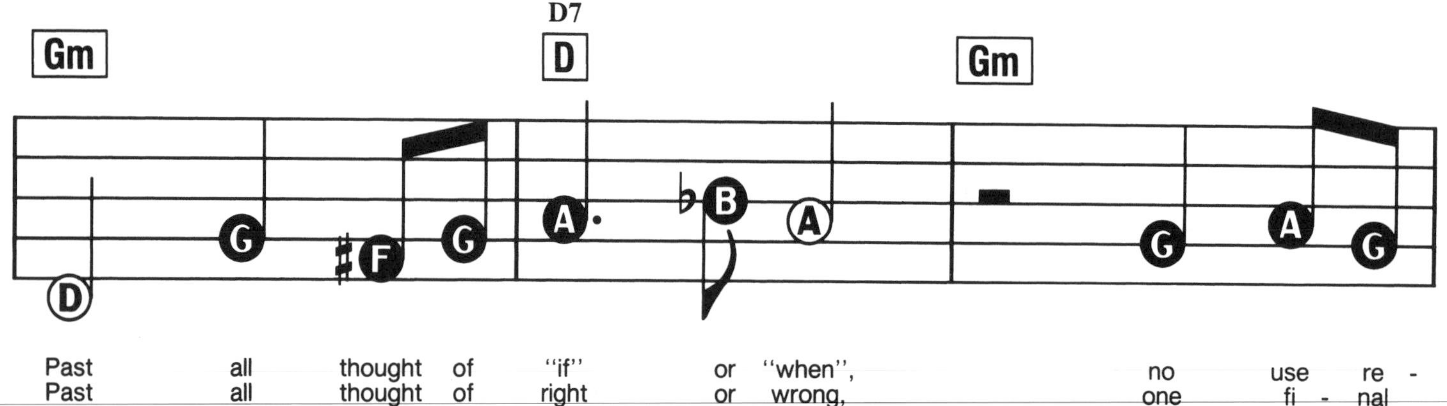
Gm
D7
D
Gm
Past all thought of "if" or "when", no use re -
Past all thought of right or wrong, one fi - nal

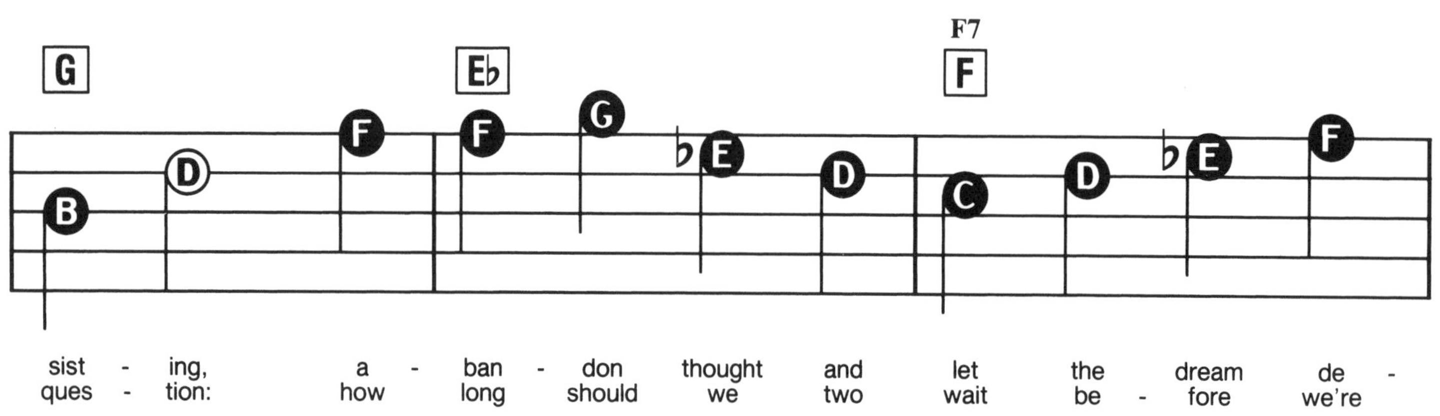
G
E♭
F7
F
sist - ing, a - ban - don thought and let the dream de -
ques - tion: how long should we two wait be - fore we're

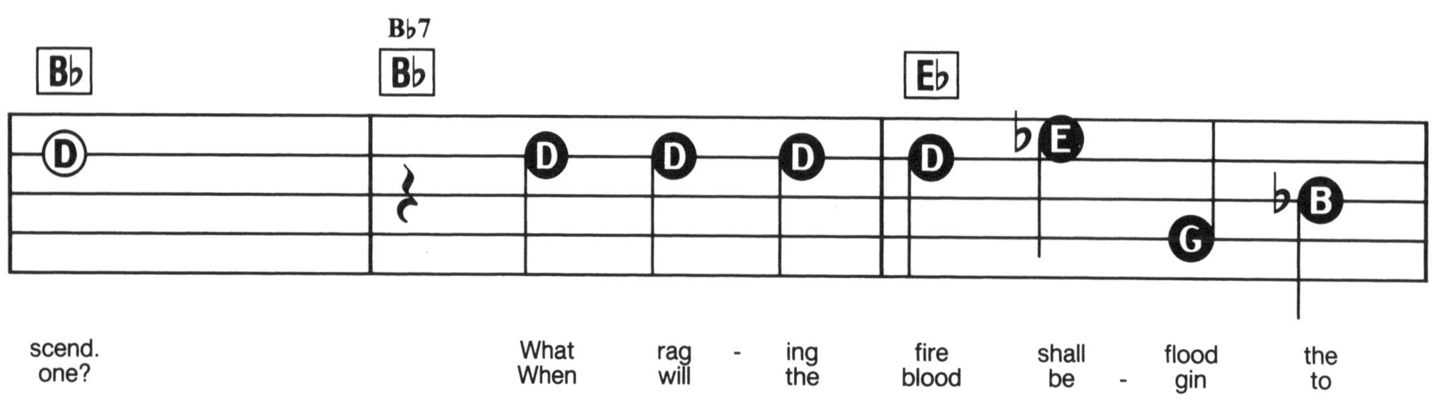
B♭
B♭7
B♭
E♭
scend. What rag - ing fire shall flood the
one? When will the blood be - gin to

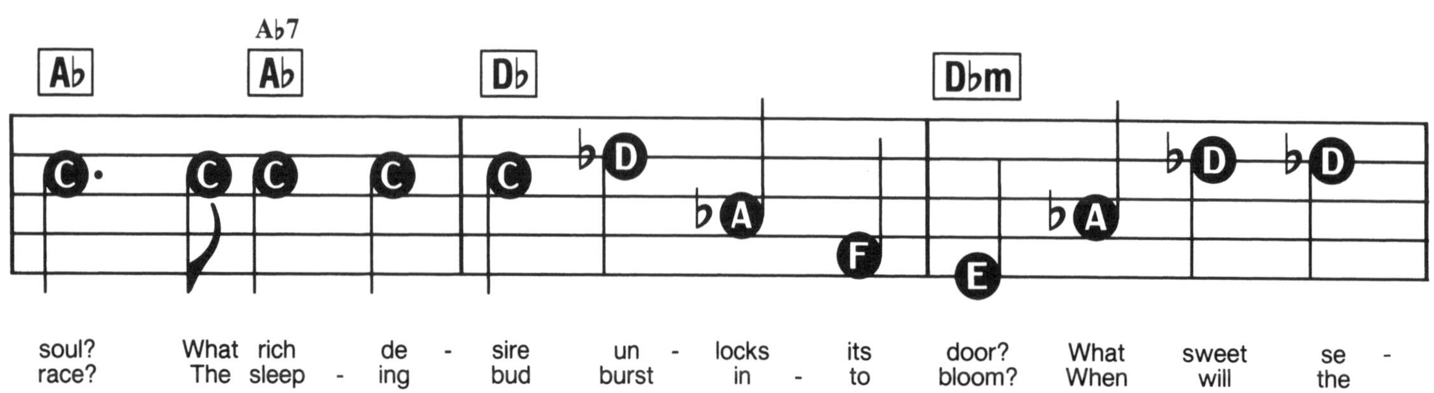
A♭
A♭7
A♭
D♭
D♭m
soul? What rich de - sire un - locks its door? What sweet se -
race? The sleep - ing bud burst in - to bloom? When will the

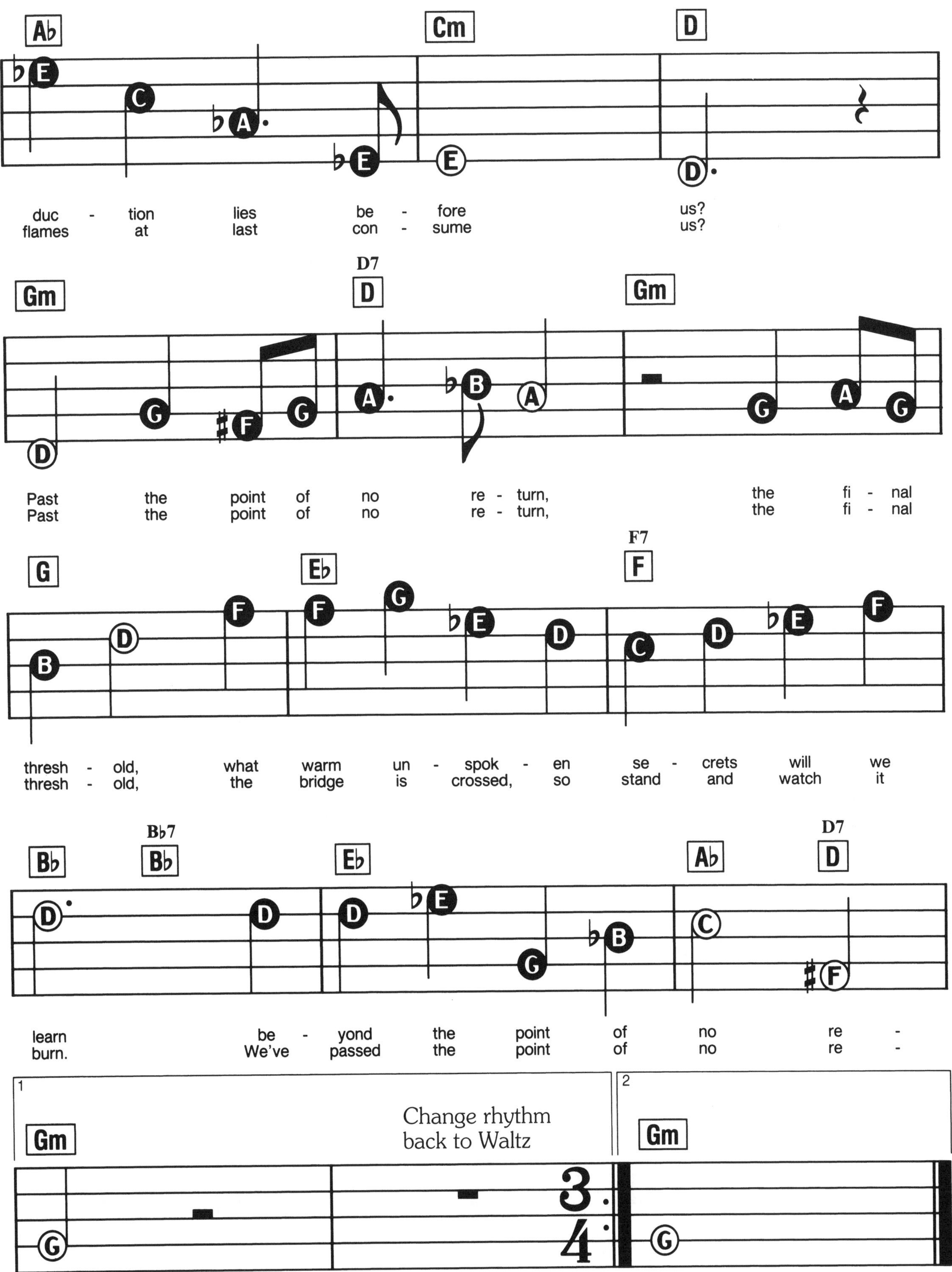
A♭
Cm
D
duc - tion lies be - fore us?
flames at last con - sume us?
Gm
D7
D
Gm
Past the point of no re - turn, the fi - nal
Past the point of no re - turn, the fi - nal
G
E♭
F7
F
thresh - old, what warm un - spok - en se - crets will we
thresh - old, the bridge is crossed, so stand and watch it
B♭
B♭7
B♭
E♭
A♭
D7
D
learn be - yond the point of no re -
burn. We've passed the point of no re -
1
Gm
Change rhythm
back to Waltz
2
Gm
turn?
turn.

Seeing Is Believing

from ASPECTS OF LOVE

Registration 10
Rhythm: 4/4 Ballad or Broadway

Music by Andrew Lloyd Webber
Lyrics by Don Black and Charles Hart

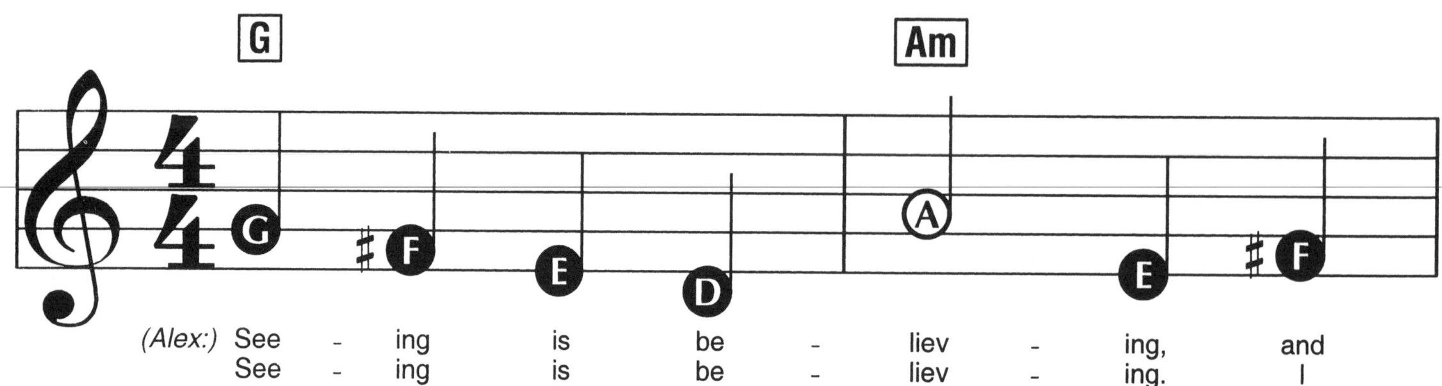

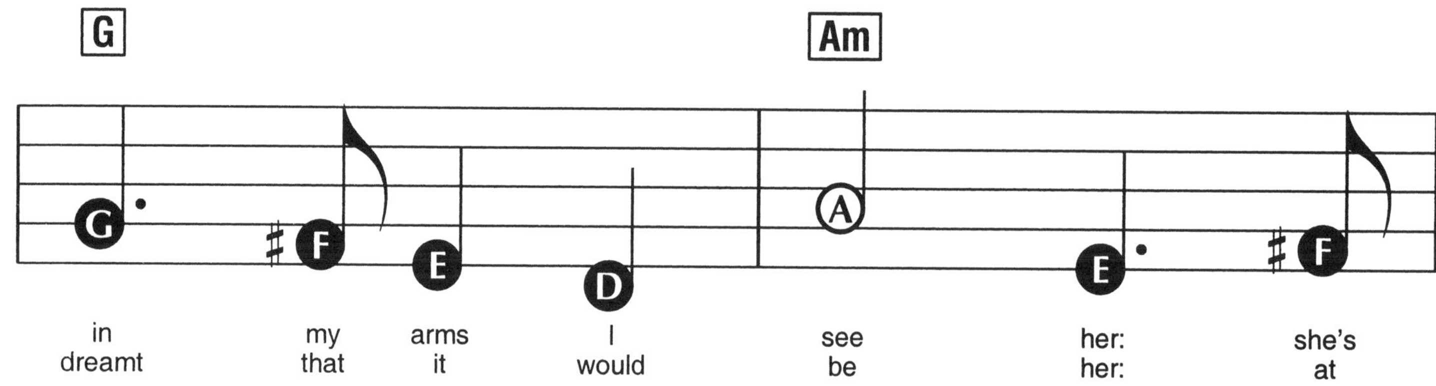

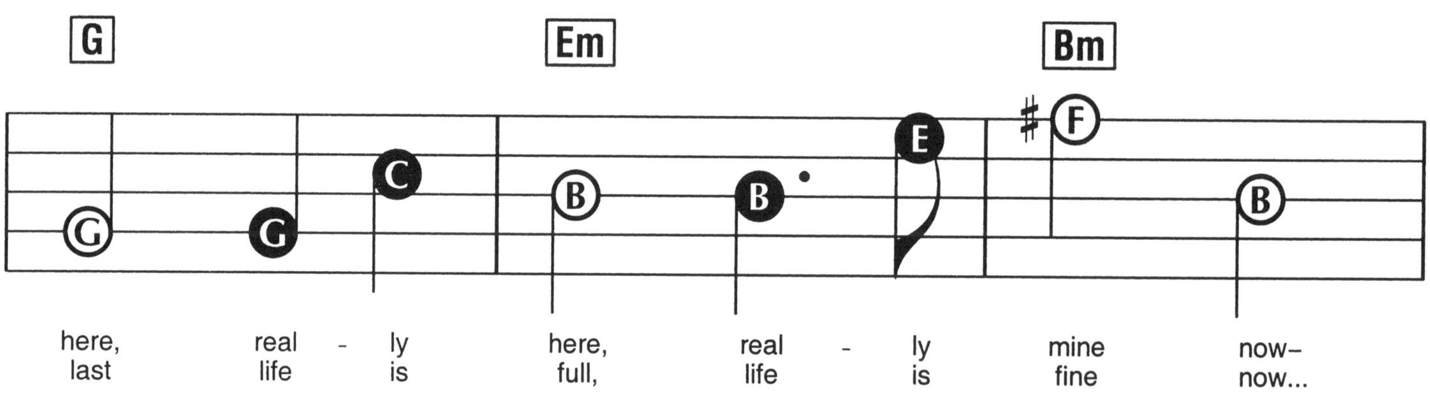

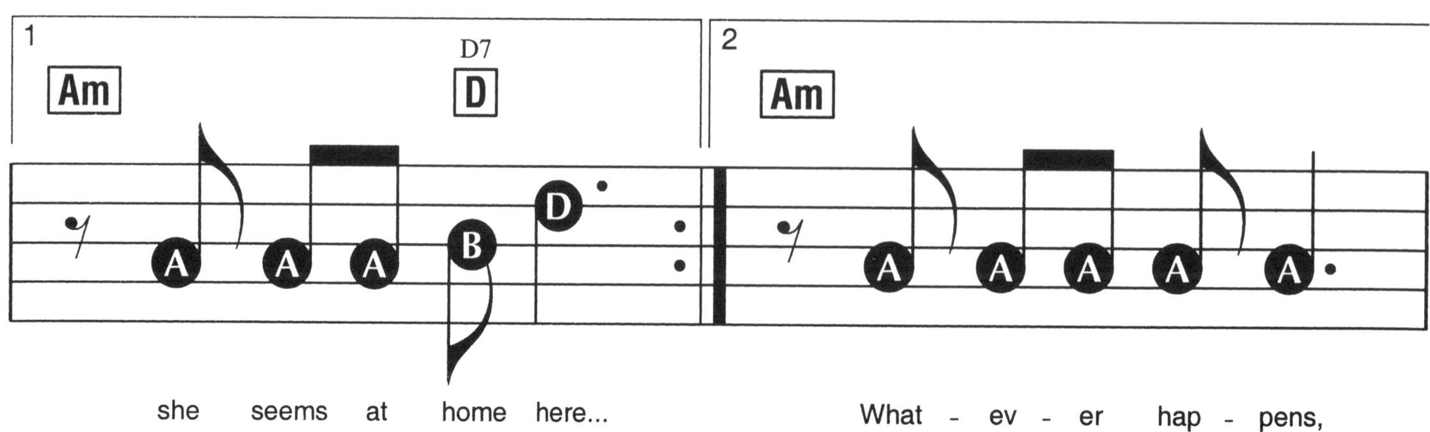

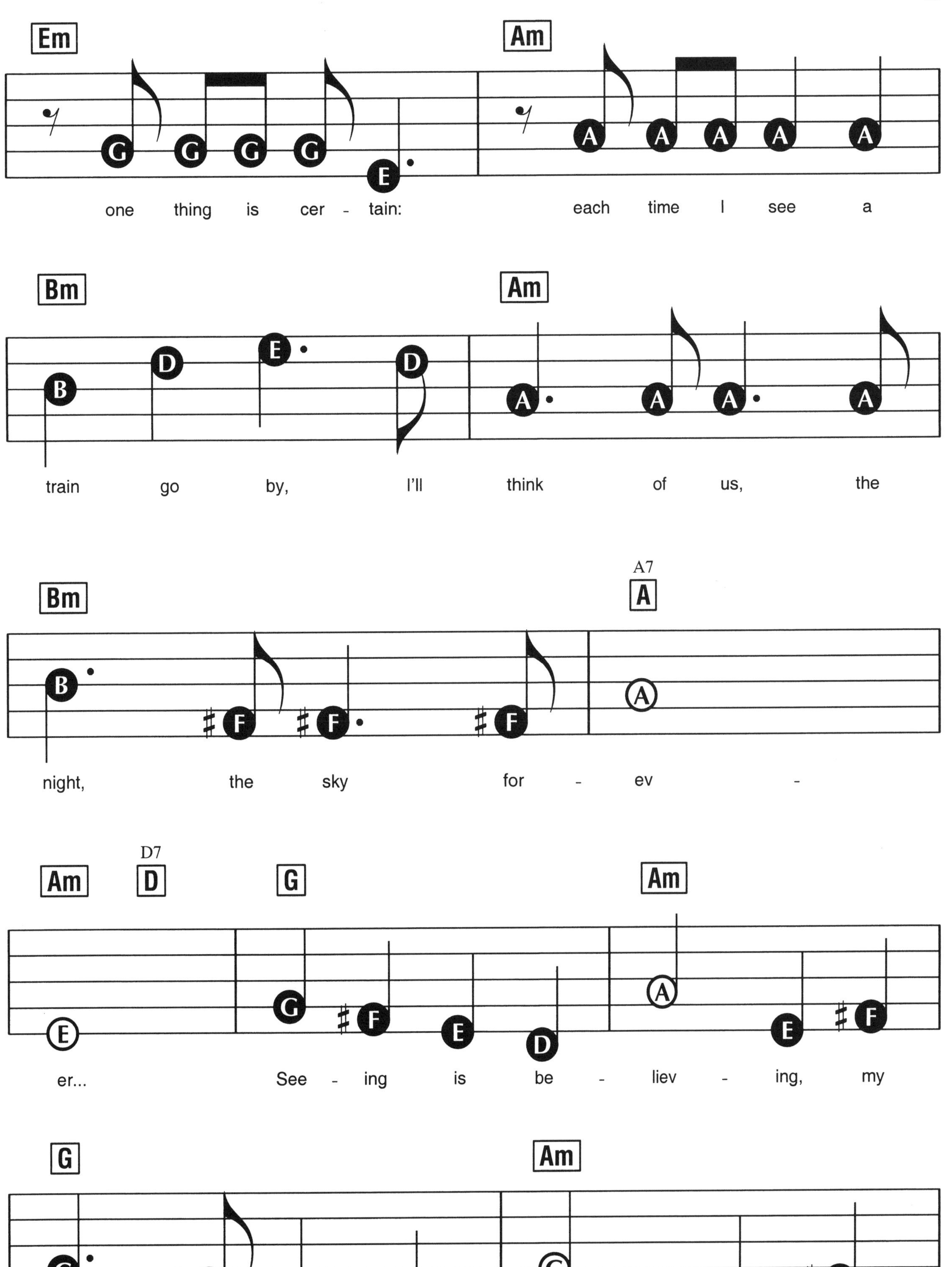
Em
Am
one thing is cer - tain:
each time I see a
Bm
Am
train go by, I'll
think of us, the
Bm
A7
A
night, the sky for - ev -
Am
D7
D
G
Am
er...
See - ing is be - liev - ing, my
G
Am
life is just be - gin - ning we

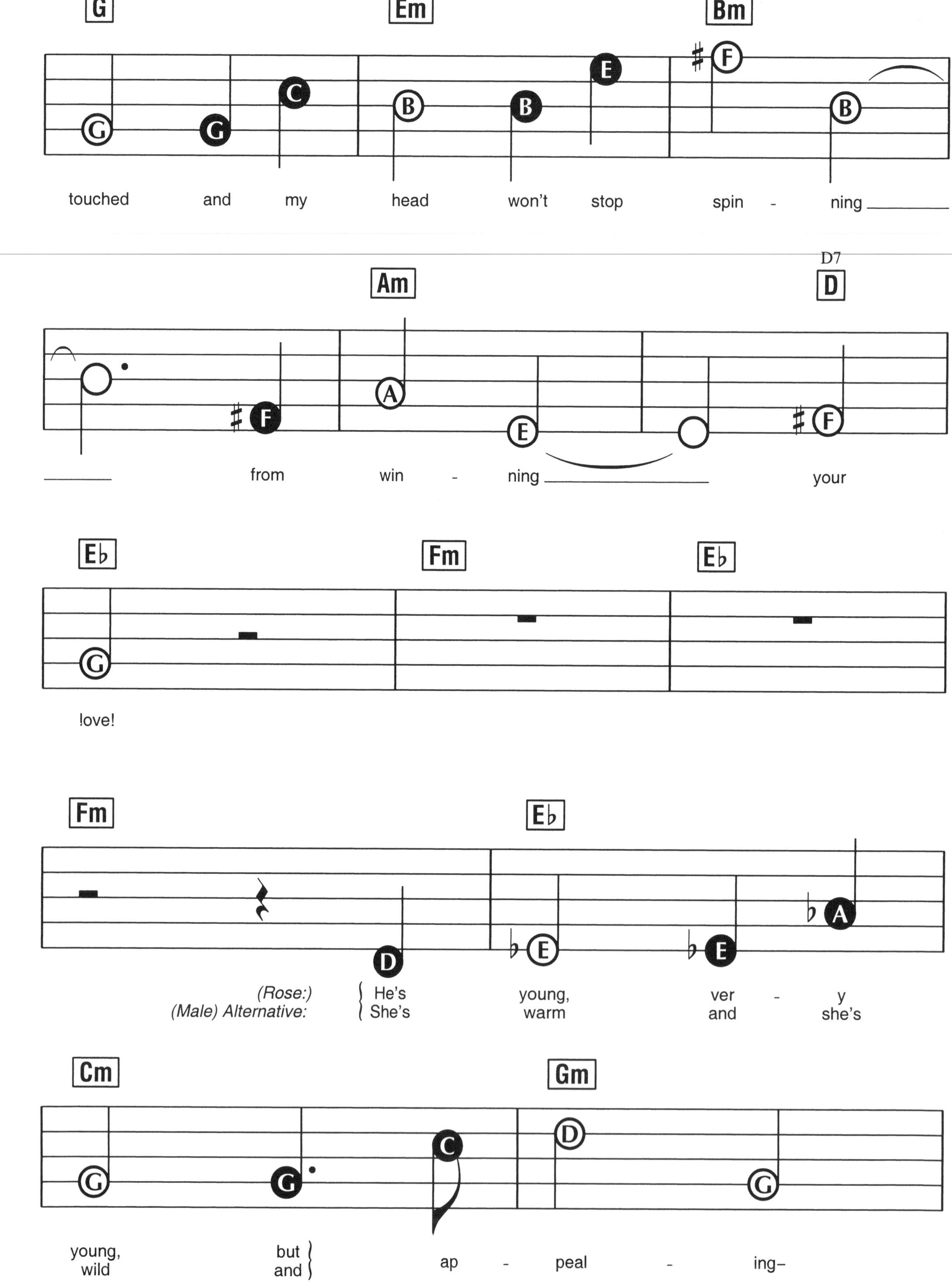
G
Em
Bm
G
G
C
B
B
E
F
B
touched and my head won't stop spin - ning
Am
D7
D
F
A
E
F
from win - ning your
E♭
Fm
E♭
G
love!
Fm
E♭
D
E
E
A
(Rose:) He's young, ver - y
(Male) Alternative: She's warm and she's
Cm
Gm
G
G
C
D
G
young, but ap - peal - ing–
wild and

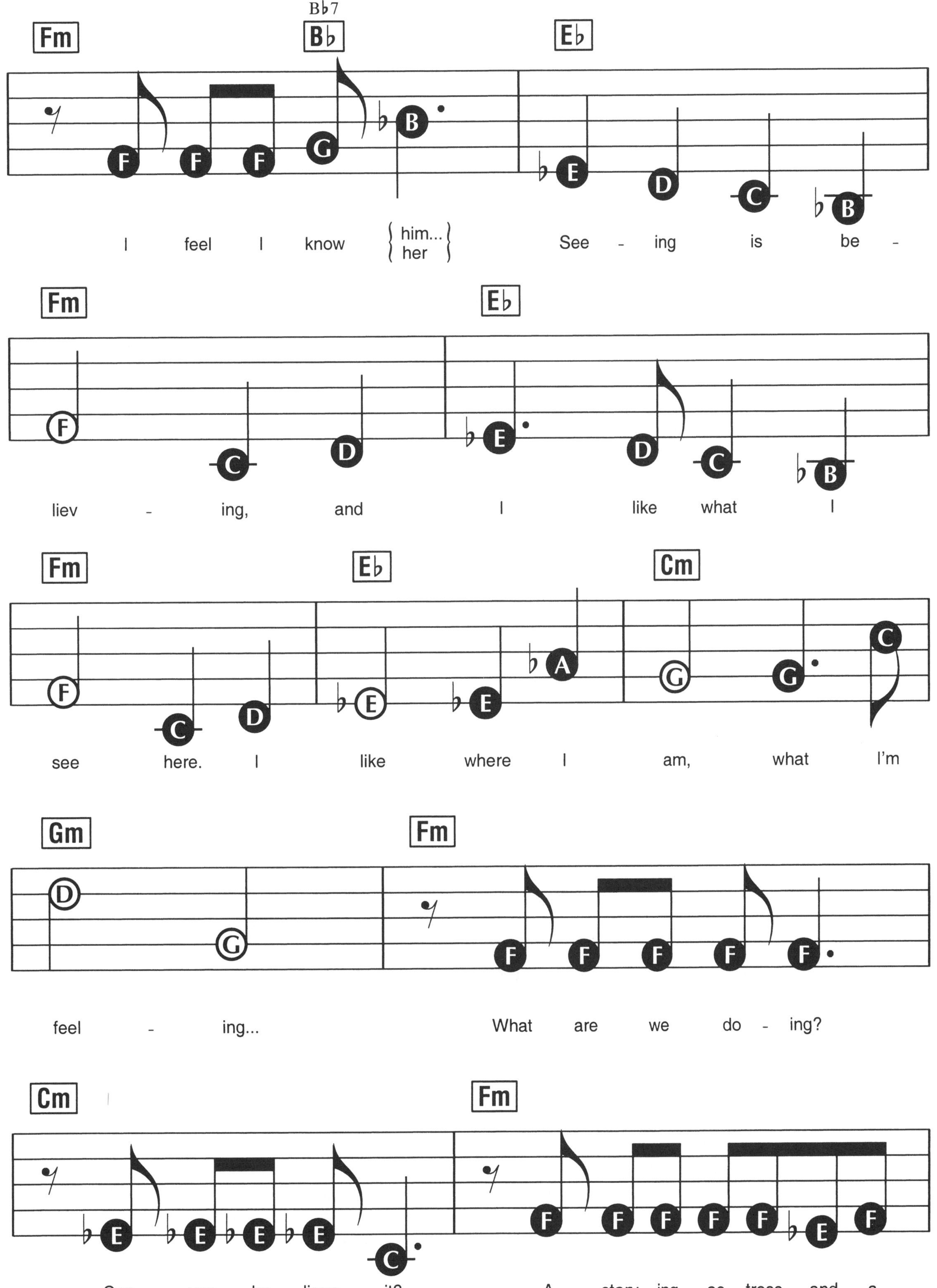
Fm
B♭7
B♭
E♭
I feel I know
him...
her
See - ing is be -
Fm
E♭
liev - ing, and
I like what I
Fm
E♭
Cm
see here. I
like where I
am, what I'm
Gm
Fm
feel - ing...
What are we do - ing?
Cm
Fm
Can you be - lieve it?
A starv - ing ac - tress and a

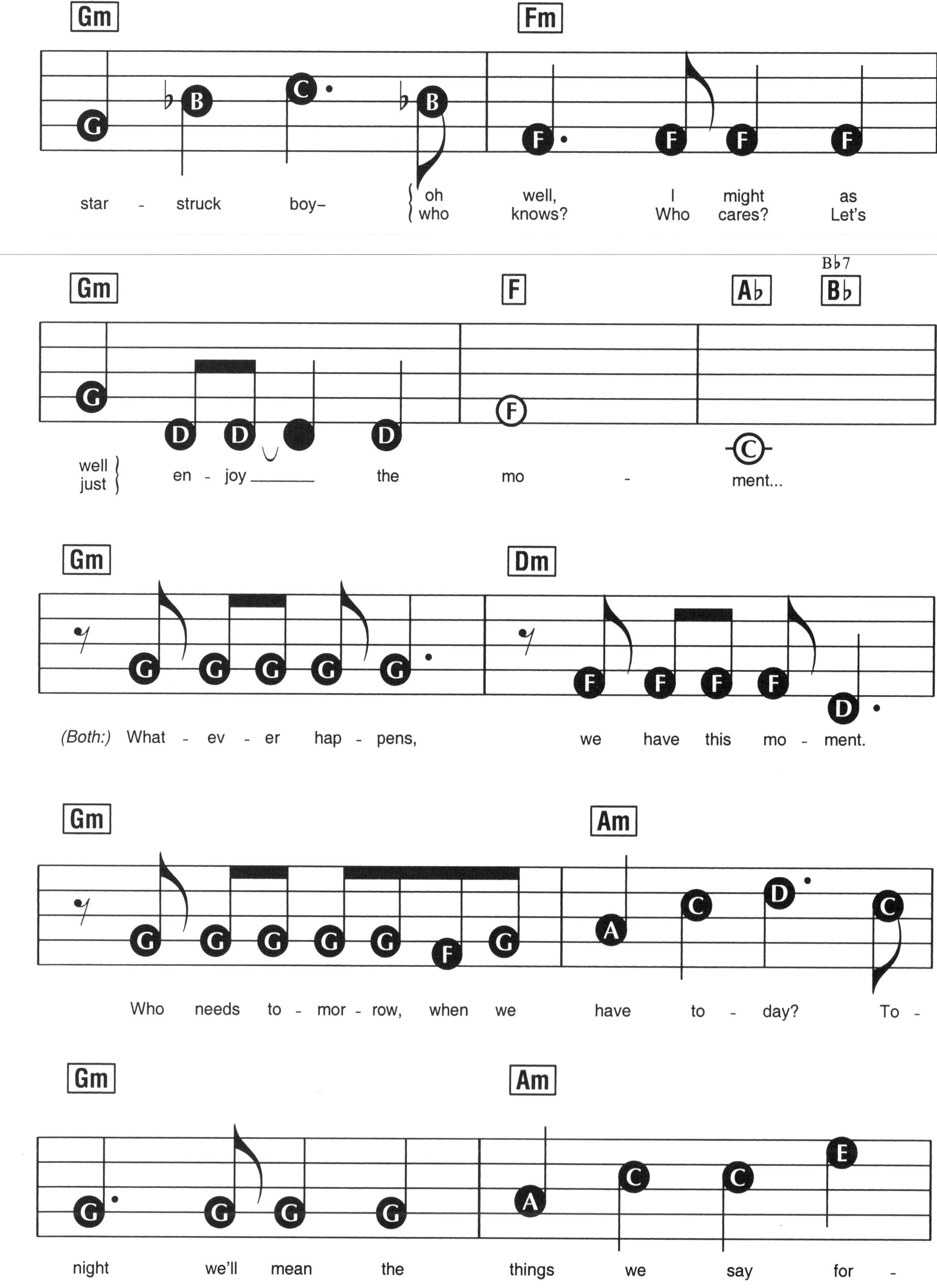
Gm
Fm
star - struck boy–
oh who
well, knows?
I Who
might cares?
as Let's
Gm
F
A♭
B♭7
B♭
well just
en - joy ___ the
mo - ment...
Gm
Dm
(Both:) What - ev - er hap - pens,
we have this mo - ment.
Gm
Am
Who needs to - mor - row, when we
have to - day? To -
Gm
Am
night we'll mean the
things we say for -

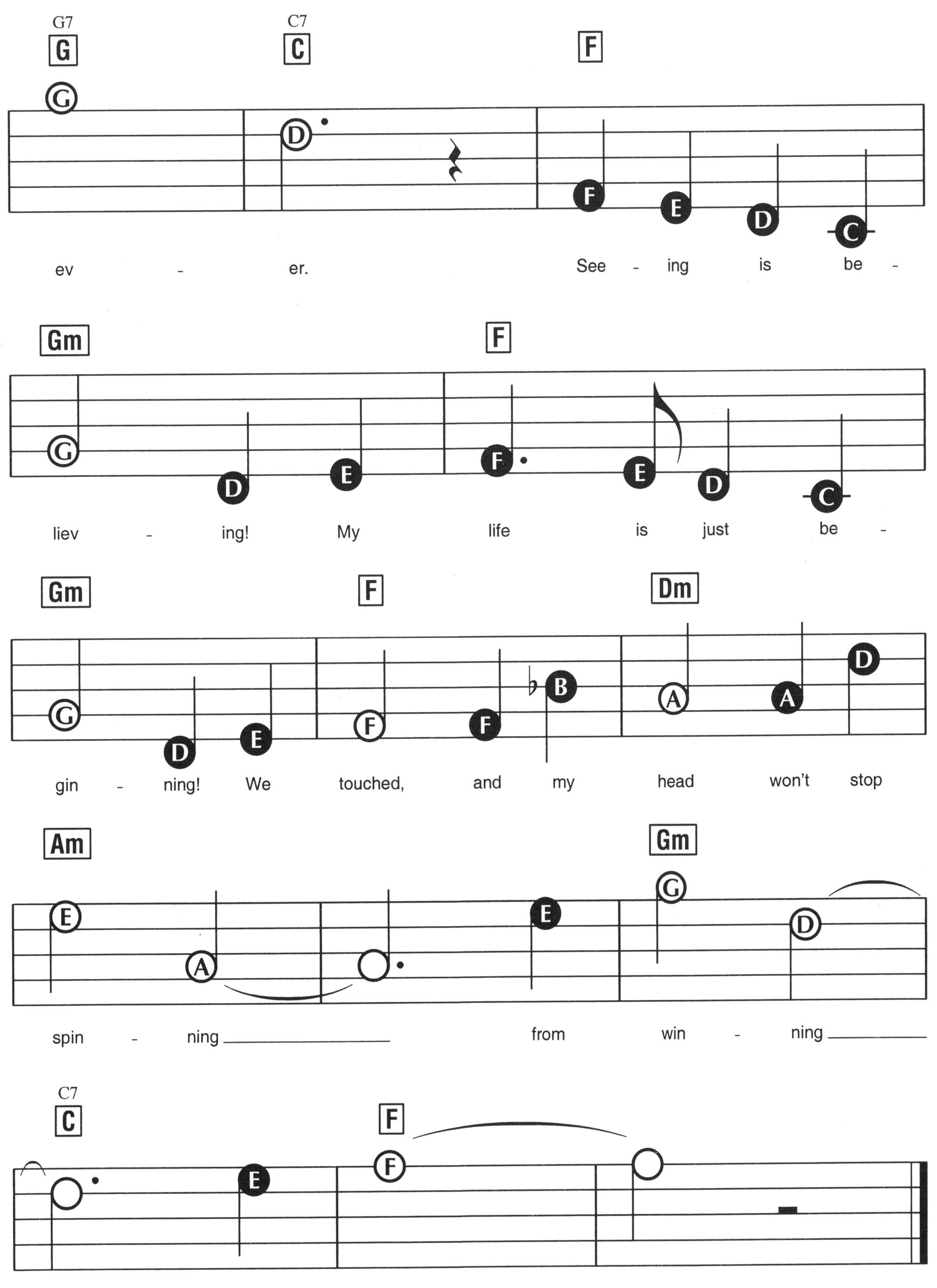
G7
G
G
C7
C
D
F
F
E
D
C
ev - er. See - ing is be -
Gm
F
G
D
E
F
E
D
C
liev - ing! My life is just be -
Gm
F
Dm
G
D
E
F
F
B
A
A
D
gin - ning! We touched, and my head won't stop
Am
Gm
E
A
E
G
D
spin - ning from win - ning
C7
C
F
E
F
your love!

Starlight Express

from STARLIGHT EXPRESS

Registration 1
Rhythm: 8-Beat or Rock

Music by Andrew Lloyd Webber
Lyrics by Richard Stilgoe

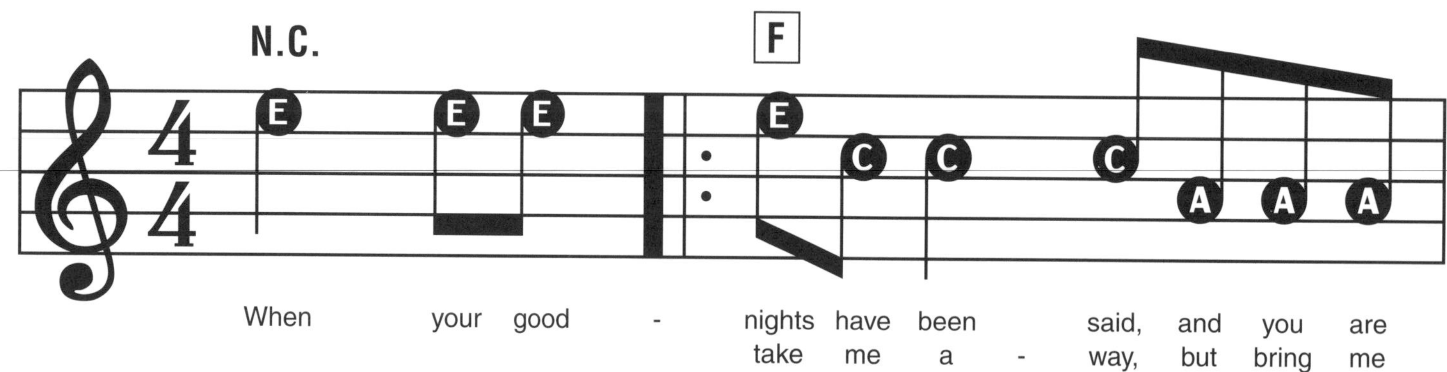
N.C.
F
When your good - nights have been said, and you are
take me a - way, but bring me

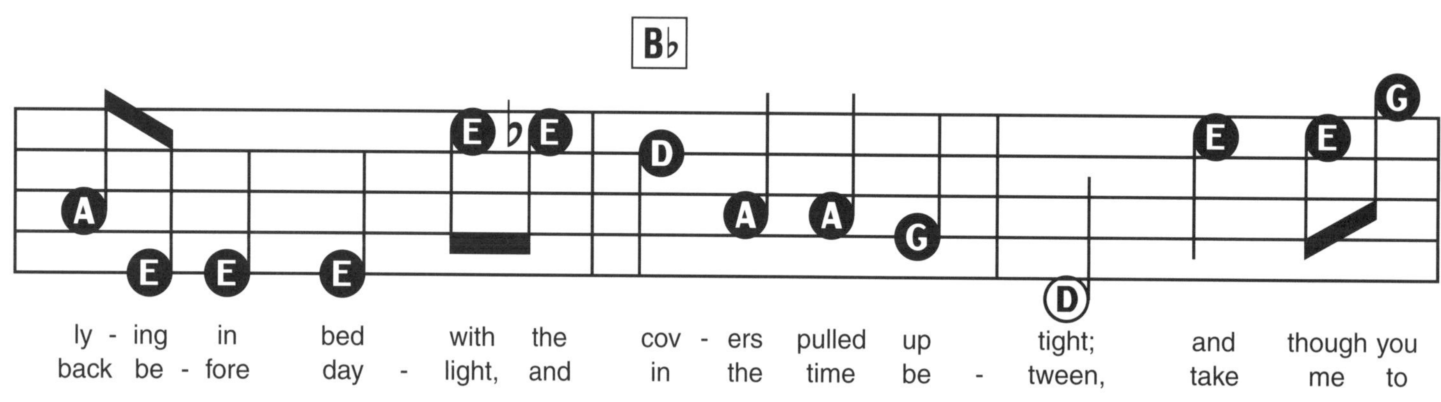
B♭
ly - ing in bed with the cov - ers pulled up tight; and though you
back be - fore day - light, and in the time be - tween, take me to

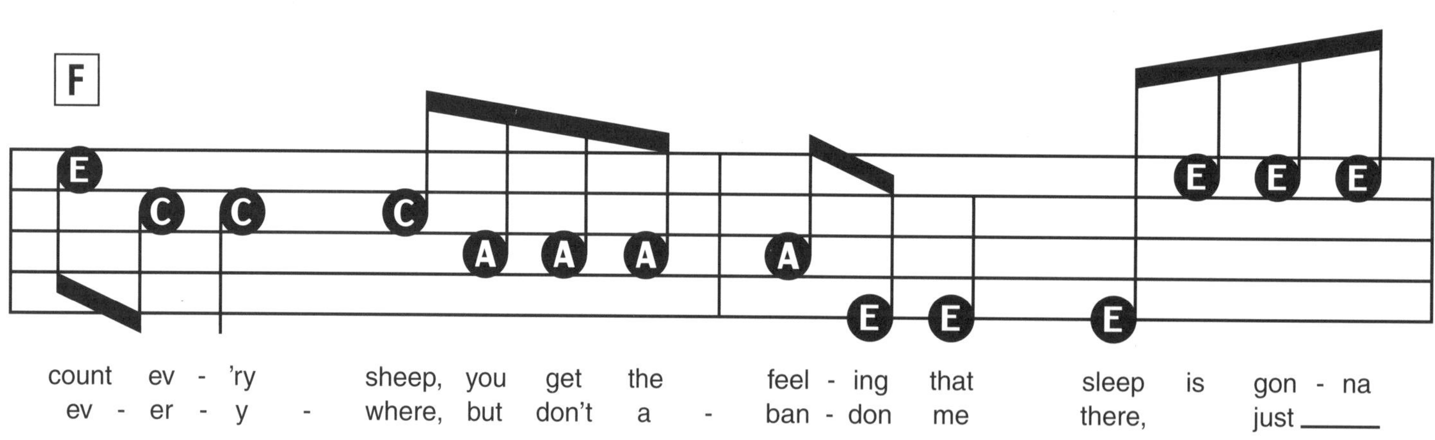
F
count ev - 'ry sheep, you get the feel - ing that sleep is gon - na
ev - er - y - where, but don't a - ban - don me there, just

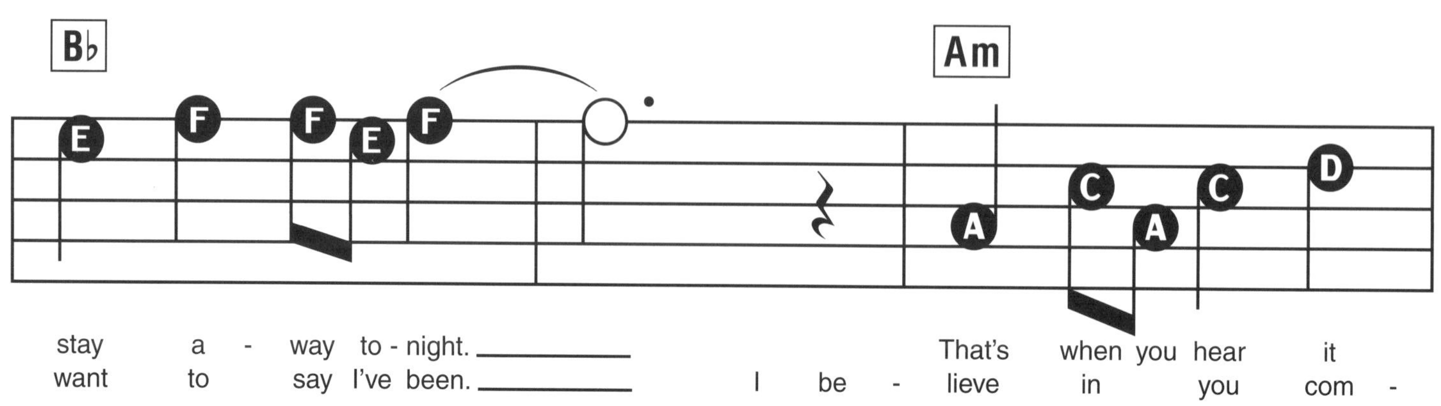
B♭
Am
stay a - way to - night.
want to say I've been.
That's when you hear it
I be - lieve in you com -

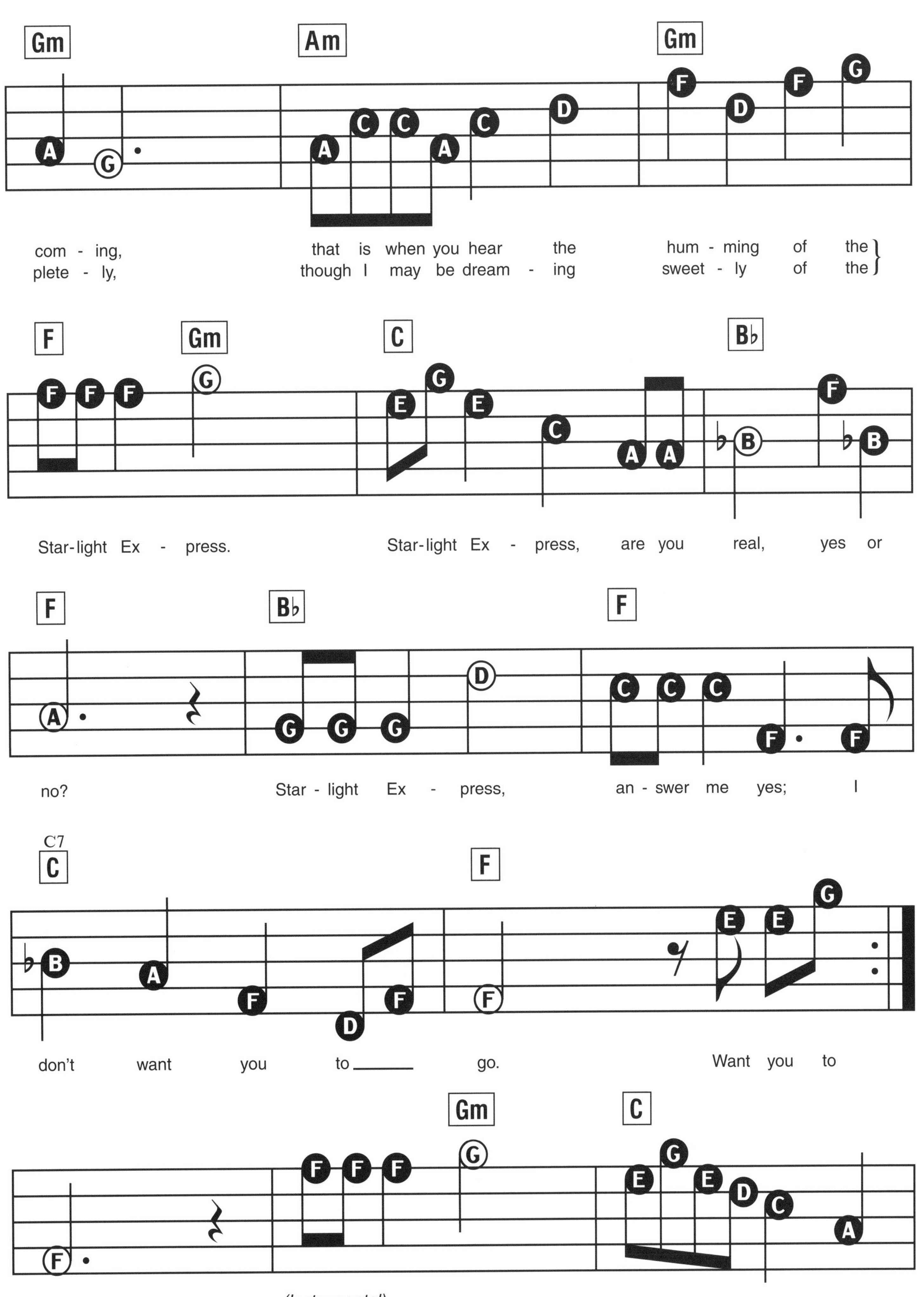
Gm
Am
Gm
A G
A C C A C D
F D F G
com - ing,
plete - ly,
that is when you hear the
though I may be dream - ing
hum - ming of the
sweet - ly of the
F
Gm
C
B♭
F F F G
E G E C A A
B F B
Star-light Ex - press.
Star-light Ex - press, are you real, yes or
F
B♭
F
A
G G G D
C C C F F
no?
Star - light Ex - press,
an - swer me yes; I
C7
C
F
B A F D F
F E E G
don't want you to
go.
Want you to
Gm
C
F
F F F G
E G E D C A
go.
(Instrumental)

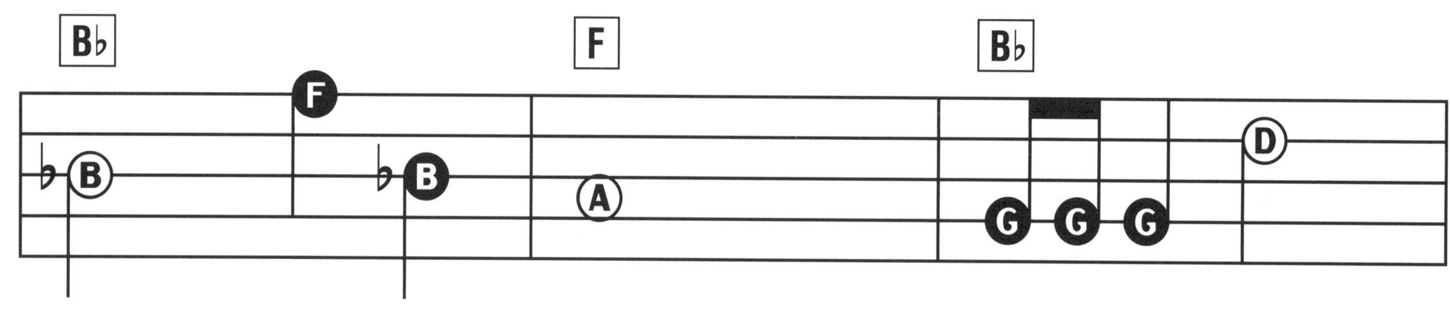
B♭
F
B
B
F
A
B♭
G
G
G
D

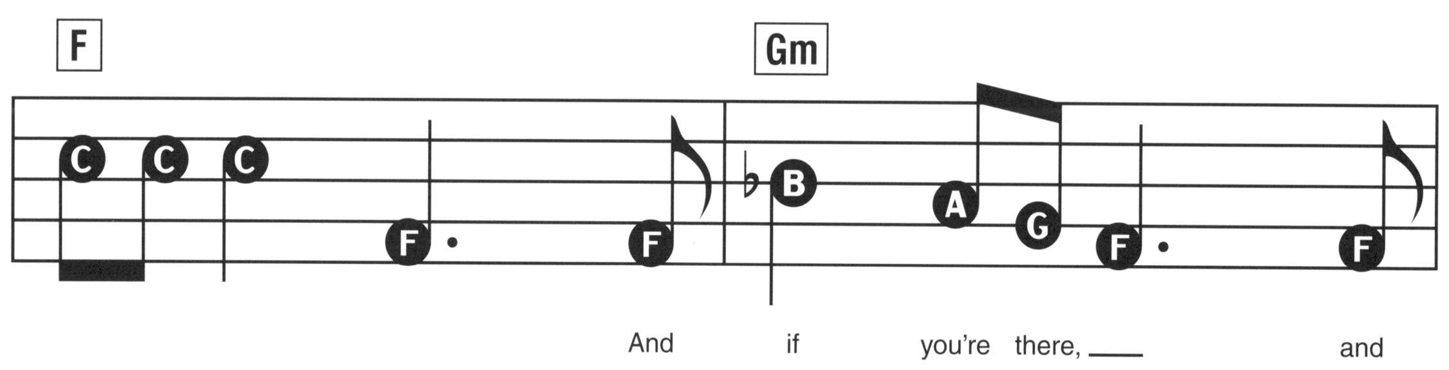
F
C
C
C
F
F
Gm
B
A
G
F
F
And
if
you're
there,
and

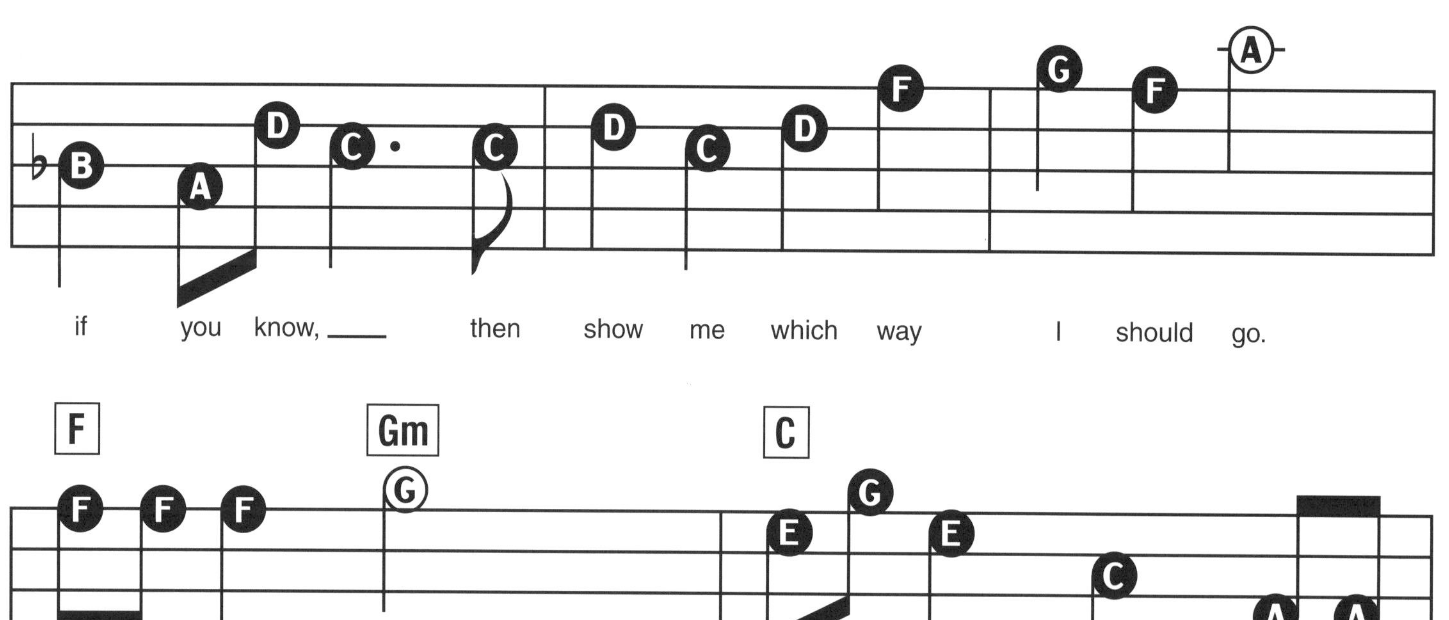
B
A
D
C
C
D
C
D
F
G
F
A
if
you
know,
then
show
me
which
way
I
should
go.
F
F
F
F
Gm
G
C
E
G
E
C
A
A
Star - light
Ex - press,
Star - light
Ex - press,
are
you

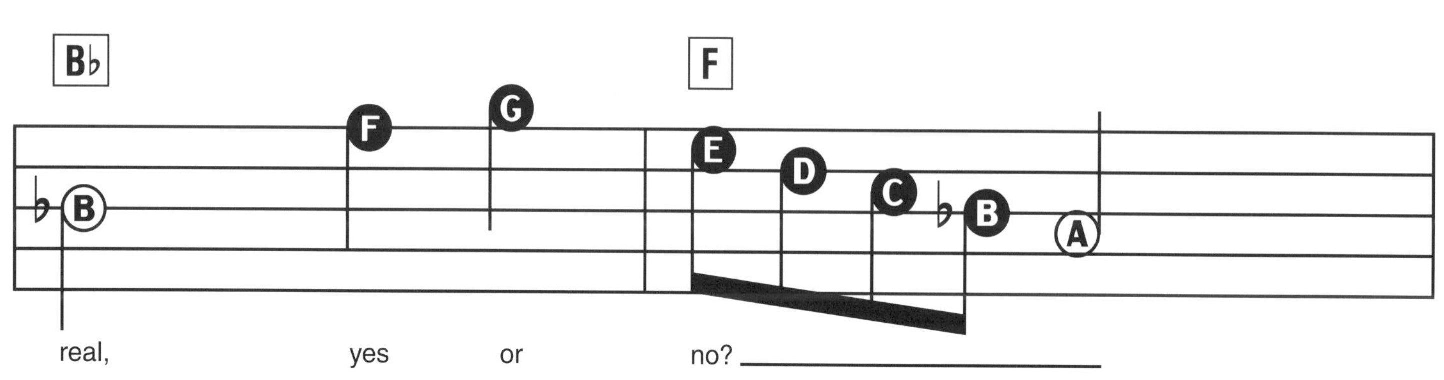
B♭
B
F
G
F
E
D
C
B
A
real,
yes
or
no?

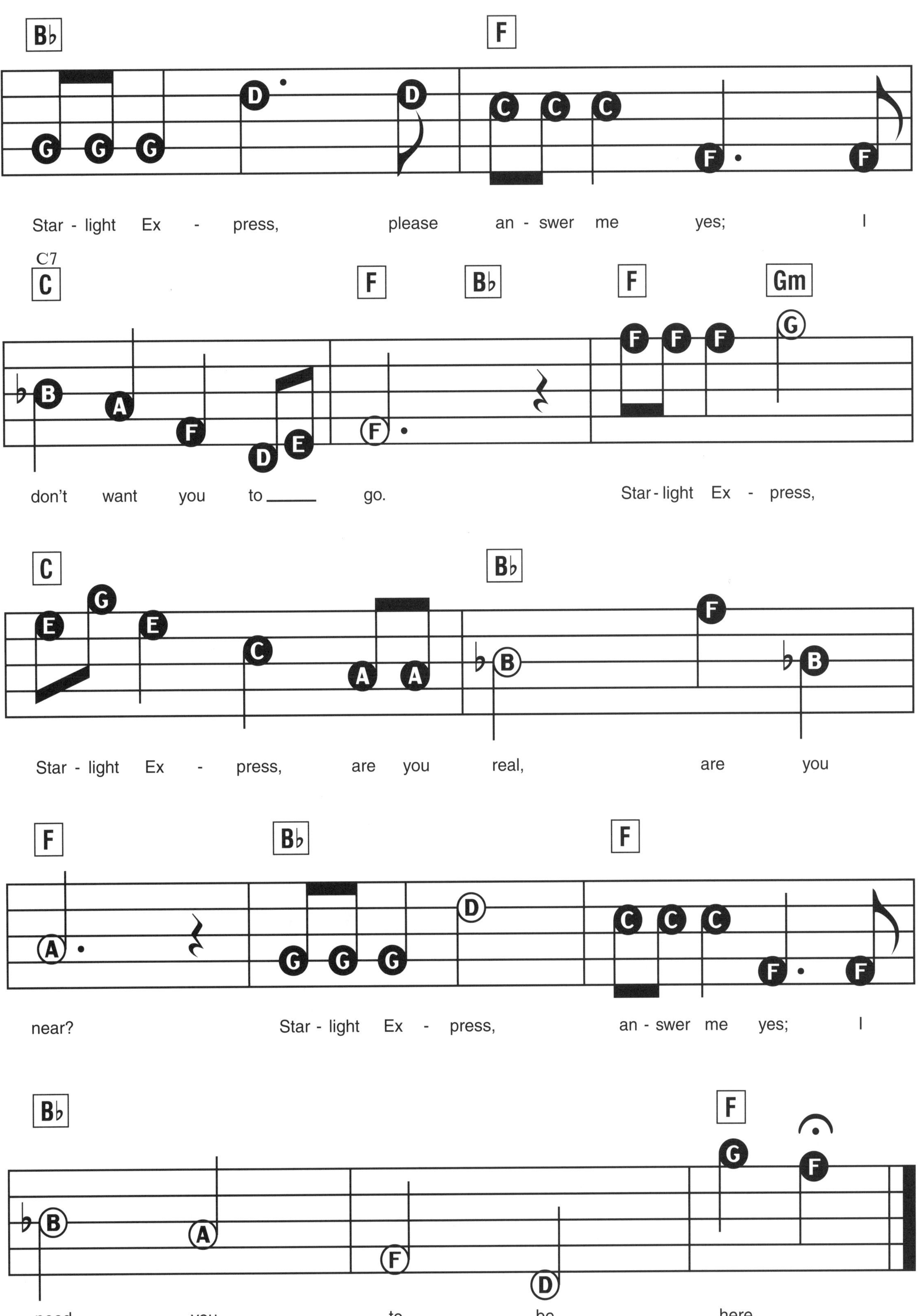

B♭
F
Star - light Ex - press, please an - swer me yes; I
C7
C
F
B♭
F
Gm
don't want you to ___ go. Star - light Ex - press,
C
B♭
Star - light Ex - press, are you real, are you
F
B♭
F
near? Star - light Ex - press, an - swer me yes; I
B♭
F
need you to be here. ___

Take That Look Off Your Face

from SONG & DANCE

Registration 3
Rhythm: 8-Beat or Rock

Music by Andrew Lloyd Webber
Lyrics by Don Black

2, 3
F
G
C
D D C C B C C D
know if he had - n't gone. Take that
on - ly a wom - an can. No, I
E D C C C D E D C C D E
look off your face. (Take that look off your face.) I can
did - n't dig deep. (No, I did - n't dig deep.) I did
G7
G
F E D D D E F E D D E F
see through your smile. (I can see through your smile.) You would
not want to know. (I did not want to know.) Well, you
C
G F E E G F E D E
love to be right, I bet you did - n't
don't in - ter - fere when you're scared of the
G7
G
F E D D F E D C D
sleep good last night, could - n't wait to bring
things you might hear. When he's back, you think

F7
F
Am
all of that bad news to my door. Well, I've
I will end it right there and then. Well, my
F7
F
To Coda
got news for you, I knew be -
fair weath - er friend, you're wrong a -
C
F
C
D.S. al Coda
(Return to
Play to and
Skip to Coda)
fore. (Instrumental) If
gain.
CODA
C
G
gain. Take that
C
look off your face. (Take that look off your face.) I can

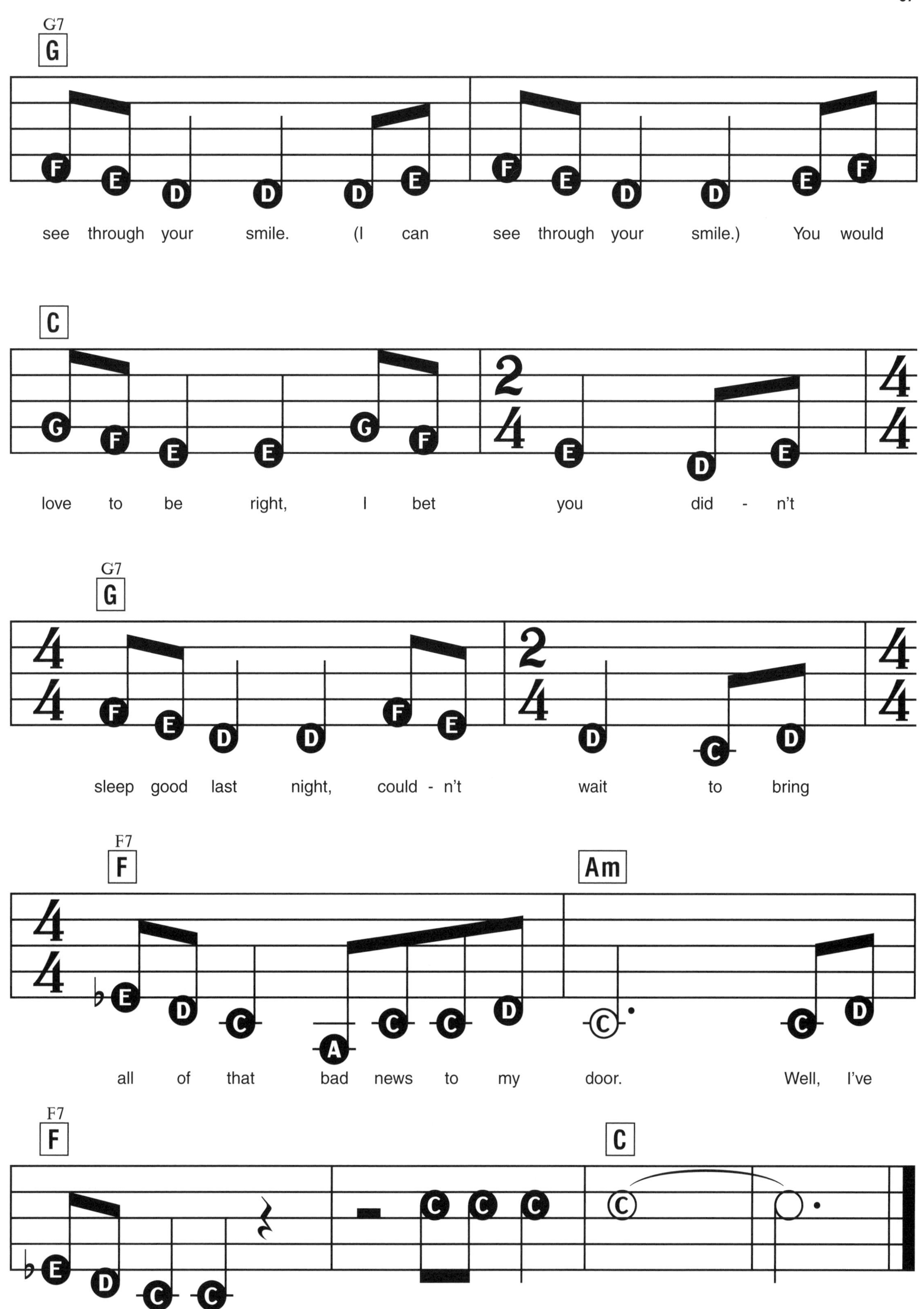
G7
G
see through your smile. (I can see through your smile.) You would
C
love to be right, I bet you did - n't
G7
G
sleep good last night, could - n't wait to bring
F7
F
Am
all of that bad news to my door. Well, I've
F7
F
C
got news for you, I knew be - fore.

Wishing You Were Somehow Here Again

from THE PHANTOM OF THE OPERA

Registration 3
Rhythm: 8-Beat or Rock Ballad

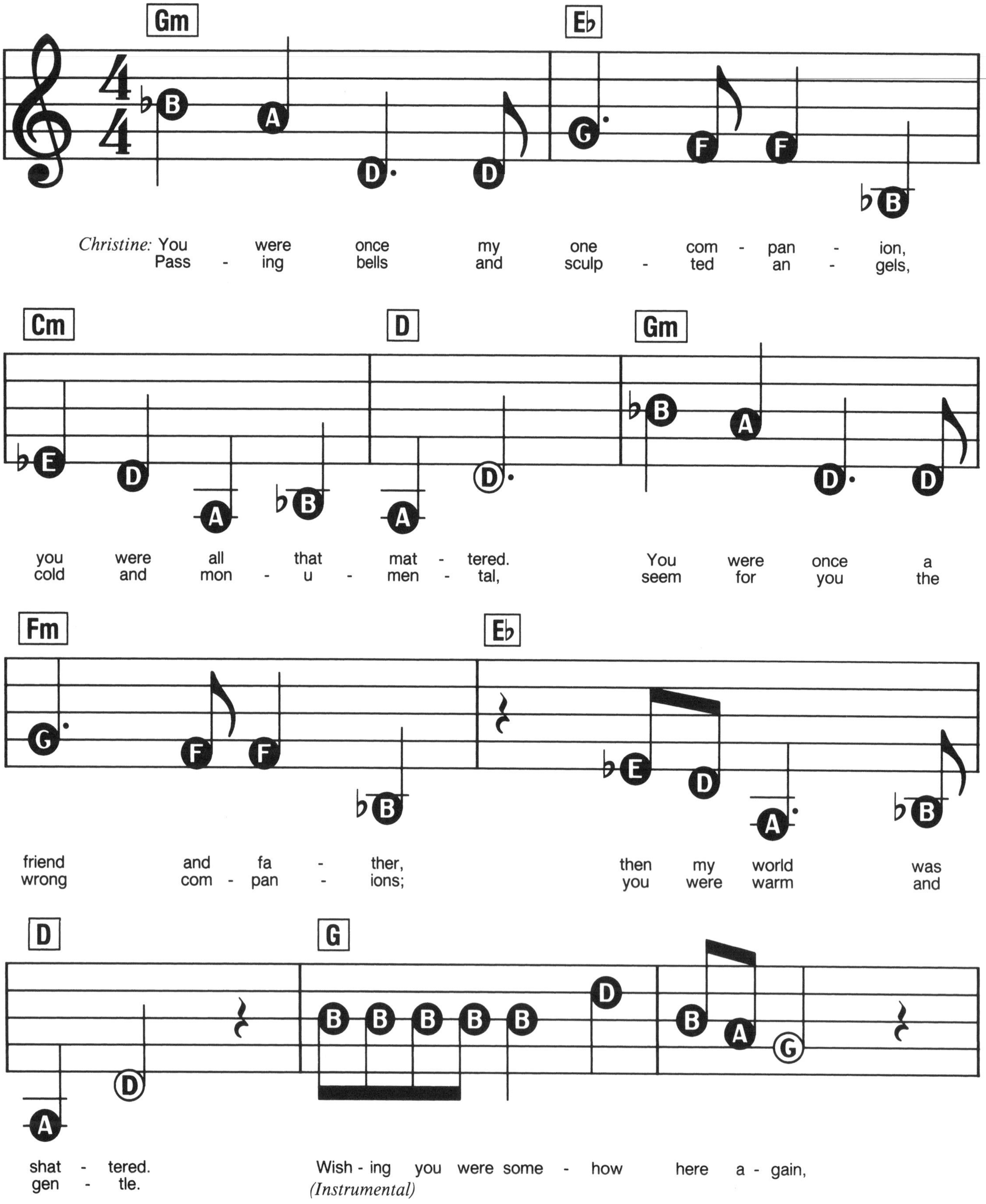

Music by Andrew Lloyd Webber
Lyrics by Charles Hart
Additional Lyrics by Richard Stilgoe

Gm Eb

Christine: You were once my one com - pan - ion,
Pass - ing bells and sculp - ted an - gels,

Cm D Gm

you were all that mat - tered. You were once a
cold and mon - u - men - tal, seem for you the

Fm Eb

friend and fa - ther, then my world was
wrong com - pan - ions; you were warm and

D G

shat - tered. Wish - ing you were some - how here a - gain,
gen - tle. *(Instrumental)*

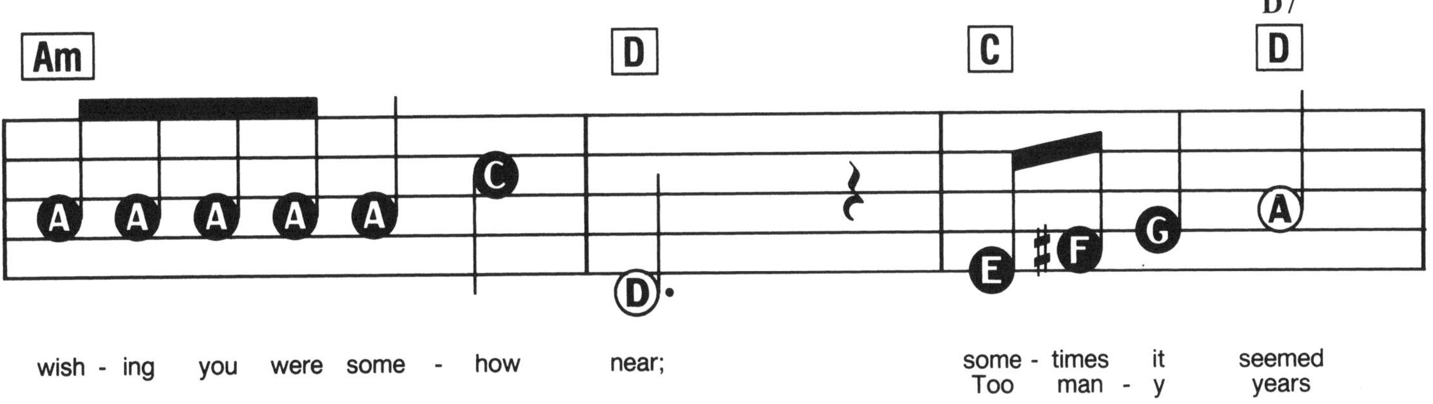
Am
D
C
D7
D
wish - ing you were some - how near;
some - times it seemed
Too man - y years

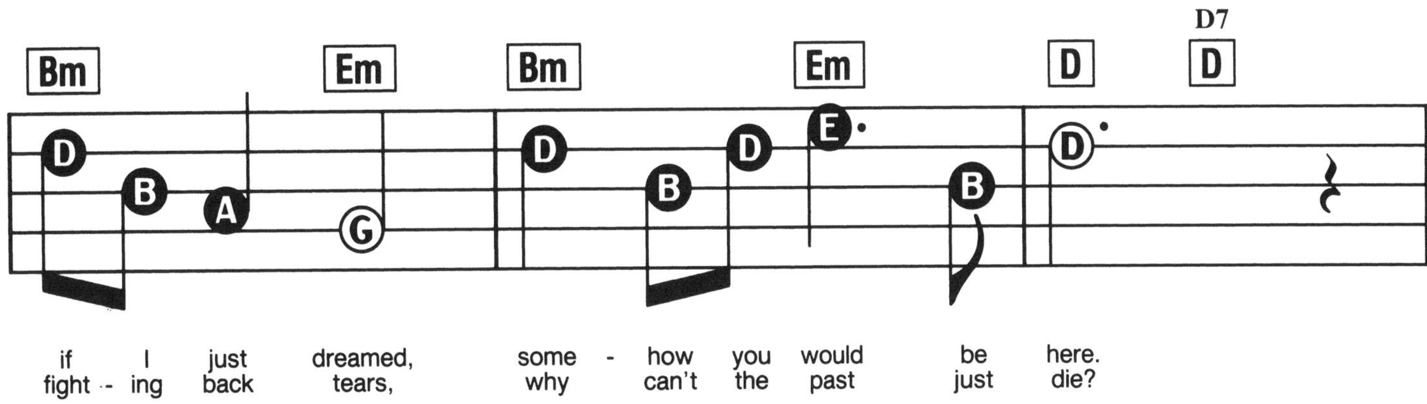
Bm
Em
Bm
Em
D
D7
D
if I just dreamed,
fight - ing back tears,
some - how you would be here.
why can't the past just die?

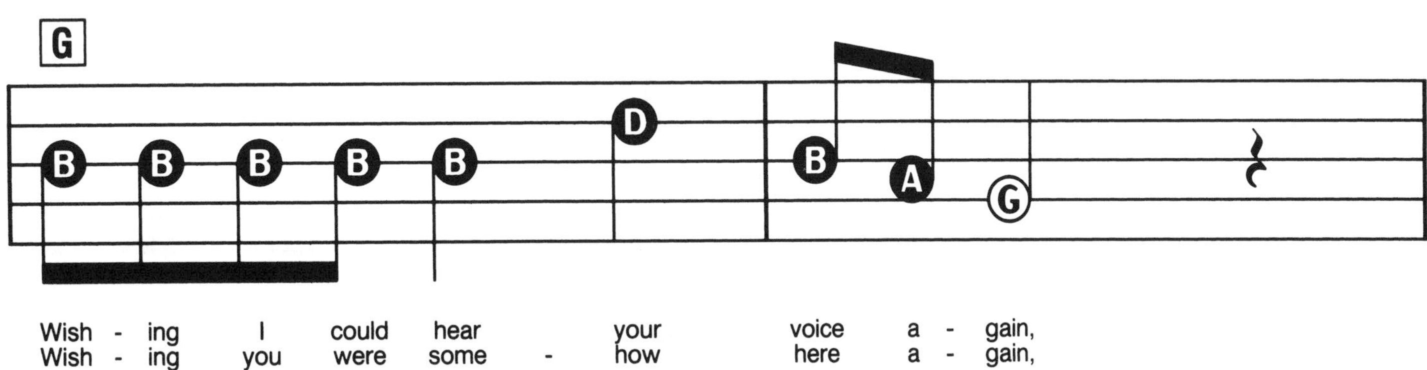
G
Wish - ing I could hear your voice a - gain,
Wish - ing you were some - how here a - gain,

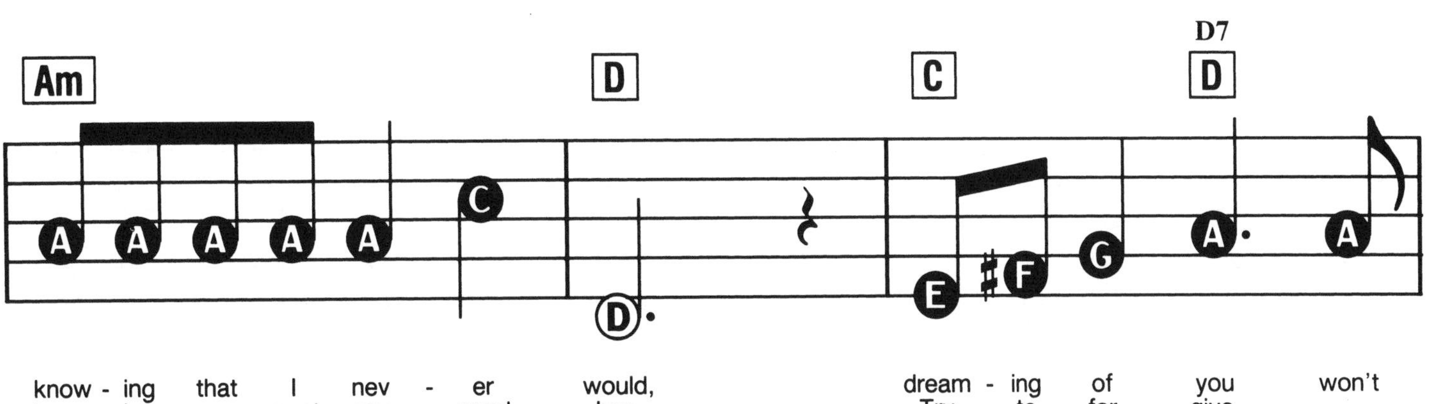
Am
D
C
D7
D
know - ing that I nev - er would,
know - ing we must say good - bye.
dream - ing of you won't
Try to for - give,

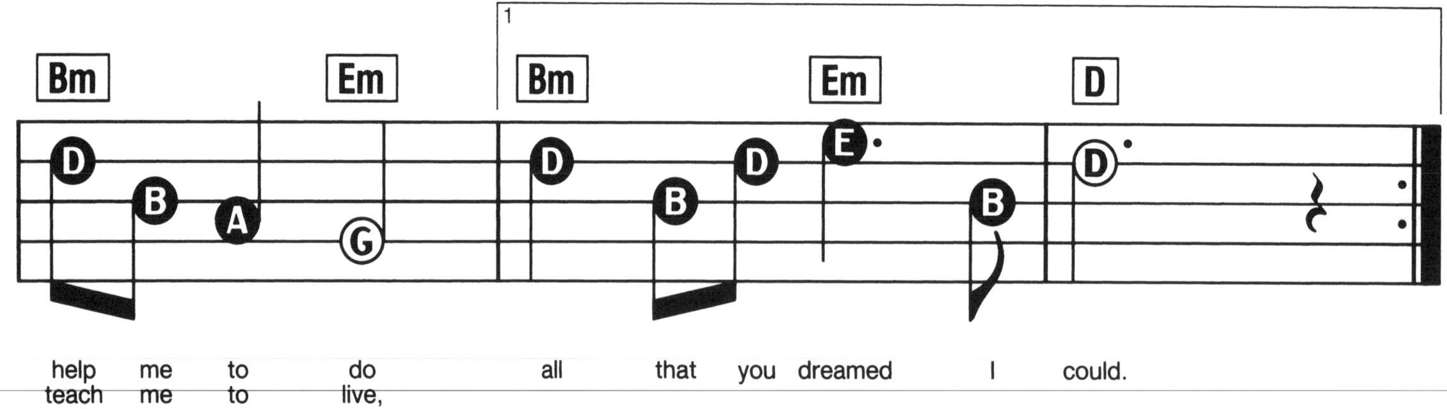
1
Bm Em Bm Em D
D B A G D B D E B D
help me to do all that you dreamed I could.
teach me to live,

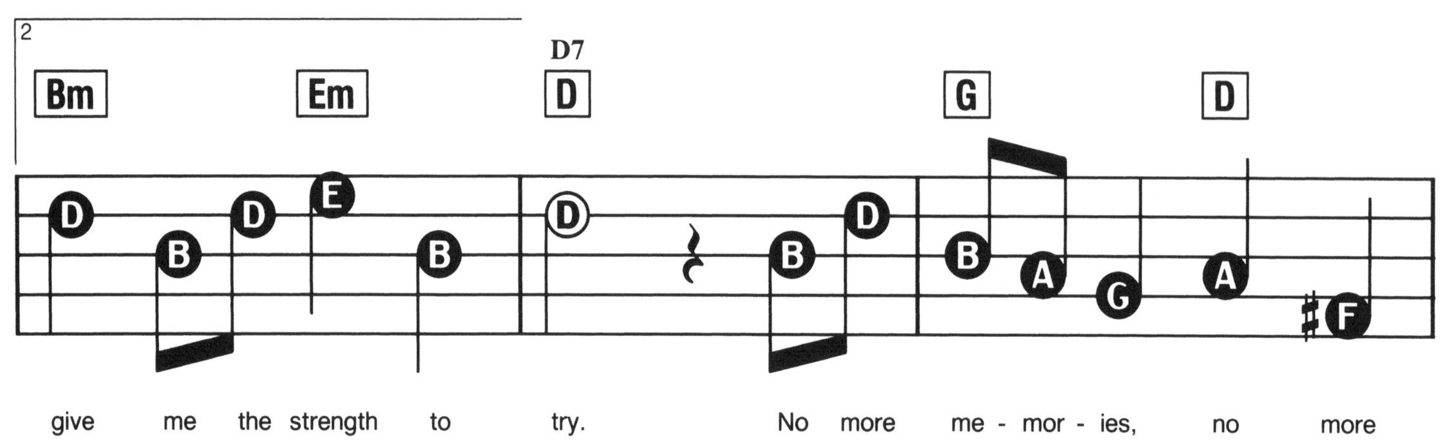
2
Bm Em D7 D G D
D B D E B D B D B A G A F
give me the strength to try. No more me - mor - ies, no more

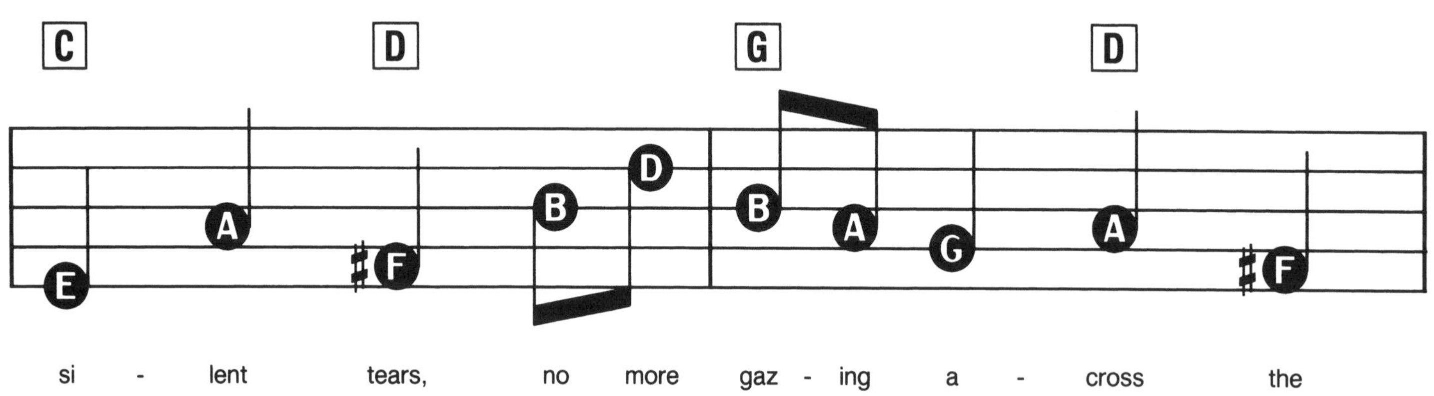
C D G D
E A F B D B A G A F
si - lent tears, no more gaz - ing a - cross the

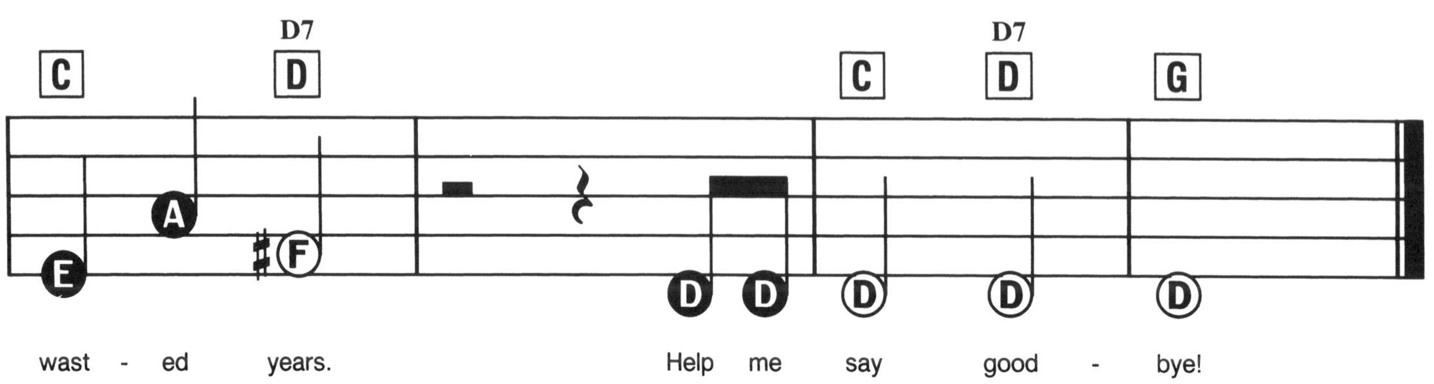
C D7 D C D7 D G
E A F D D D D D
wast - ed years. Help me say good - bye!

Registration Guide

• Match the Registration number on the song to the corresponding numbered category below. Select and activate an instrumental sound available on your instrument.

• Choose an automatic rhythm appropriate to the mood and style of the song. (Consult your Owner's Guide for proper operation of automatic rhythm features.)

• Adjust the tempo and volume controls to comfortable settings.

Registration

1	Mellow	Flutes, Clarinet, Oboe, Flugel Horn, Trombone, French Horn, Organ Flutes
2	Ensemble	Brass Section, Sax Section, Wind Ensemble, Full Organ, Theater Organ
3	Strings	Violin, Viola, Cello, Fiddle, String Ensemble, Pizzicato, Organ Strings
4	Guitars	Acoustic/Electric Guitars, Banjo, Mandolin, Dulcimer, Ukulele, Hawaiian Guitar
5	Mallets	Vibraphone, Marimba, Xylophone, Steel Drums, Bells, Celesta, Chimes
6	Liturgical	Pipe Organ, Hand Bells, Vocal Ensemble, Choir, Organ Flutes
7	Bright	Saxophones, Trumpet, Mute Trumpet, Synth Leads, Jazz/Gospel Organs
8	Piano	Piano, Electric Piano, Honky Tonk Piano, Harpsichord, Clavi
9	Novelty	Melodic Percussion, Wah Trumpet, Synth, Whistle, Kazoo, Perc. Organ
10	Bellows	Accordion, French Accordion, Mussette, Harmonica, Pump Organ, Bagpipes